# MANDY'S GOURMET SALADS

*recipes for lettuce and life*

# MANDY'S GOURMET SALADS

*recipes for lettuce and life*

By Mandy Wolfe, Rebecca Wolfe and Meredith Erickson

appetite
by RANDOM HOUSE

Appetite by Random House® and colophon are registered trademarks of Penguin Random House LLC.

Library and Archives Canada Cataloguing in Publication is available upon request.
ISBN: 978-0-525-61047-2
eBook ISBN: 978-0-525-61048-9

Photography by Alison Slattery, Two Food Photographers
Photo on page 60 by photographer, Mikaël Theimer and photo on page 186 by by Michelle Little Photography
Design by Cow Goes Moo
Printed and bound in China

Published in Canada by Appetite by Random House®, a division of Penguin Random House Canada Limited.

www.penguinrandomhouse.ca

10   9   8   7

appetite
by RANDOM HOUSE

*This book is dedicated to our families: those we were born into, those we are making, and those we have chosen. And in honor of our late father, Jason Wolfe, for instilling in us his vibrant entrepreneurial spirit, and for always being our biggest fan.*

# Contents

Us (Mandy, left and Rebecca, right) with Vince (center)

# Our Story

The story of Mandy's is a story of two sisters (that would be us, Mandy and Rebecca!), and so it really begins with our story. We'll let Rebecca start it:

REBECCA | When I was a student at Parsons in New York in the late 90s, the New York salad-bar scene was at its apex. On every corner, there was a generic chopped salad place—whatever the epitome of "healthy lunch made easy" was at the time. I tried a lot of them, but nothing tasted as good as what my sister Mandy made for me when we were growing up in Montreal. While I was in New York, I would fantasize about her monster chopped salad with garden-fresh herb vinaigrette. Or her cilantro and mint–rich salad, inspired by her travels through Vietnam in her early 20s, or her real specialty: the famous (huge) chocolate chip cookies she'd been making for our entire family since she was young.

I was 19 at the time, and my boyfriend (now husband) Vince had a clothing shop called Mimi & Coco back in Victoria Village in Montreal where, as a summer job, I sold clothes. Vince had a little space in the back of the shop that he wanted to convert into an Italian-inspired panini and coffee shop. The same winter we fell in love, I convinced him that the salad trend I was seeing in New York could take off in Montreal—and that instead of panini and coffee, Mimi & Coco should have a salad cafe; that Mandy would create a delicious menu for it; and that she and I would run it! Shockingly, he agreed. Then (even more shockingly) I convinced Mandy to quit her teaching job and embark on this crazy salad journey with me.

MANDY | And that is exactly what happened. In May 2004, we opened Coco Café. It was a tiny space, just 200 square feet overall, with only a three-foot counter to prep all of our salads from. Rebecca and I were the only employees. Some days we would stand behind the counter for hours and only a few customers would come in. But we believed in our product, and we stuck to our vision, and slowly word spread. We would cook the meat needed for our salads at night in our apartments—no one wants to spend $200 on a sweater that smells of curried chicken!—and bring it to the shop in the morning. We made all the dressings at night too, in batches, using our idiosyncratic expiry dating/tagging system. Our shared Jetta had a constant aroma of roasted chicken and balsamic reduction!

It took a couple of years before the lines began to snake outside of the store, but snake they did. We were bursting at the seams, and we worked our asses off. We banged out thousands of salads behind that counter and closed shop every day when we legitimately ran out of lettuce, so needless to say, our hours varied! A day in the life consisted of waking up before Aubut (Distribution Alimentaire)—a no-frills warehouse of sorts that caters to every restaurateur and café owner in Montreal—opened their doors at 7 a.m. so we could be the first ones there, then driving over Mount Royal—Montreal's cherished landmark that separates the east and west ends of the city—to our butcher in Mile End, followed by a stop at Marché Central for any other missing ingredients, all before opening the café in time for our first customers to arrive. I don't know how many times we made sesame syrup reduction at 2 a.m. after a heavy night out and miraculously remembered

INEYARD 8 MI

Old Montreal
location

the recipe to a T! Or how many custom salads we ran out to swanky SUVs double-parked on Sherbrooke Street, lest we miss a sale or not deliver top customer service to our VIPs. After a decade of tossing salads and washing dishes at the speed of light in Coco Café, we developed carpal tunnel—even salad slinging has its health risks!

REBECCA | Coco Café was our incubator: during that time we figured out what salad combinations worked and what didn't. We were very lucky to have incredibly loyal, patient, and open-minded customers who stuck with us. And we would whip up whatever people wanted to eat. We got to know all our regulars' orders by heart. If lots of customers were asking for similar things, we knew they were onto something, and we'd officially add a new salad to the menu and name it after them! So when Brian walked through the door and asked for his favorite salad combination, Mandy made it for him. Not long after that, college students and moms and their kids and their friends would come in and say, "I want the Brian salad," and we would make Brian's favorite, and that's how some of our salads evolved. Others came straight from Mandy, like our Roman and Tuscan salads, which started with her spontaneously whipping up a sun-dried tomato pesto chicken stuffed with buffalo mozzarella on the barbecue one night for a bunch of friends. Or the Endless Summer salad, which she tipped over the edge by adding pomegranate seeds (and later, our in-house-devised Mock Chicken).

We switched the name of our business a couple of times in the early years too, changing from the original Coco Café (after we got a letter from Chanel's legal department!), to Greens & Co., which sounded too clinical and cold. Then I convinced Mandy that we should be branded with her name. For me, it has always been about Mandy's salads. Mandy would still make my salad for me every day, and I would always tell my friends and family that I was eating a "Mandy's" salad. It rolled off the tongue nicely, and I strongly believed the authenticity of it would help propel our business, simply because well, it was a true story, and Mandy was actually there. Back then we didn't know what the business would become of course, but Mandy finally accepted it after a lot of convincing. She had no idea that her name would later be on stores across the city! Today, she still asks me if I want to change the name to "Becca's" or some kind of hybrid of our names. But the name Mandy's is just right, and it's what we will always be.

BOTH | After settling on our name, we created little stickers with the first Mandy's logo, designed by our then and current fabulous graphic designer Sarah Lazar of Cow Goes Moo. And we slapped them on each and every salad container we sold. All of those customers walking around Victoria Village with their Mandy's containers marked the birth of our brand.

Fast forward to 2020, and we now have eight locations in and around the Greater Montreal area. We're still at the back of Mimi & Coco, of course, but we are also in bigger complexes, like the old Montreal Forum, and in stand-alone locations, like our gorgeous flagship in the Old Port. And we have grown our business from two employees to 400! Still, it never ceases to amaze us that it's not just our aunts and uncles and friends who are supporting us, but real Montrealers—from young professionals to multiple generations of families—and visitors to the city, who all come out to eat our food in our spaces.

The level of gratitude and awe we feel about this will never decrease. It's a beautiful feeling to look back at the past 15 years—and forward to, hopefully, many, many more.

XO Mandy & Rebecca
Spring 2020

# Wolfe Pack

MANDY | When we were growing up, the kitchen was the place to be. That's where we had our most intimate talks, our funniest moments, where we shared our challenges and wins of life. Family was and still is everything to us. No matter what, the four kids in our family (our "Wolfe Pack") were always home for dinner with our mom and dad, Judy and Jason. Every Wednesday, our mom's mom Nana would also come over for dinner, and we'd break out the British sherry and make a classic old-school recipe of hers—like shepherd's pie or chicken "à la fantaisie"—and of course a delectable dessert. Then when the weekend came, we were all up north in our family cabin together, leaving straight from school every Friday afternoon in the wood-paneled Jeep Grand Wagoneer.

Our Wolfe Pack spans 10 years in age: our eldest sibling, Jessie, is 10 years older than our youngest sibling, Josh, with me and Rebecca in the middle. Maybe Becca and I bonded over our shared middle-child position, or maybe our very different personalities were drawn to each other as we got older. When you're 10 and your little sister is 5 (or 15 and she's 10), it's a world of difference! But in our later teens and early 20s, we really meshed, becoming very close and never fighting. Which is still true to this day. Becca is all passion, warmth, good feelings, a party girl with a colorful imagination, and a perfectionist in everything she does. I, on the other hand, am a bit more laid back and quiet, more of an observer than a conversationalist. But don't be fooled by the quiet, there's always a lot going on upstairs!

The core of Mandy's has always been family. You know when you're a kid, and you set up a lemonade stand, and each of your family members has a job? That was us at the beginning: even our brother Josh was out front handing out smoothie samples for a while.

Fast forward to today, and family and food are still at the center of our lives. Raising seven kids between us, I am still overcome by loving feelings and warm memories (both familiar old ones, and the new fun ones we are making with our own kids) when we all get together for a Sunday evening meal. To watch our kids play together, and run around our restaurants after one another; to watch them help cook in the very same kitchen we grew up cooking in with our mom (up north in the Laurentians), never ceases to blow me away. It reminds me time and again what a blessing family is.

Mommy and Daddy, at our childhood home

The two of us, circa 1984

All of us, on vacation in Key Biscayne, Florida (our mom was the photographer!)

# Our Salads

What sets Mandy's apart from all the other salad joints out there?

A lot. But mostly: ratios and top-quality everyyyything—plus very caring staff and the ambience of our locations (more on that later). We're essentially a salad lab, one with weekly creative meetings where we try all the new flavor combinations of the season and also retest our current menu items. We're always thinking about ratios, both in the balance of our dressings and for our salads as a whole (e.g., no sogginess!).

It's really easy to f*#♯k up the ratio of a salad (too soggy, too much acid, too bitter), so getting it right is something we spend a lot of time on. Our general rules? Well, texturally, we like to make sure there are equal parts creaminess (avocado in almost every salad, or a nice soft cheese!), crunchiness (pita, tortilla, toasted nuts or seeds, or a crunchy vegetable), tartness—either from citrus (lemon or lime) in the salad dressing or tangy fruit in the salad (pomegranate seeds, pear, apple, cranberries)—and always—always—fat (olive oil, mayonnaise, egg, cheese, nuts, or, yes, avocado again).

Our flavor combinations are often globally inspired, but whenever we can, we use local and organic ingredients (almost always). We have a special "Monthly Salad" every month, and these are always in line with the seasons. During our Canadian winter months for example, we use fewer tomatoes and berries, but we ramp up on pears, apples, pumpkin, kale, and of course root vegetables like sweet potatoes, beets, squash, leeks, garlic, and fennel. And we crave our grain bowls (more about those on page 173) and farro and seeds to keep us going through those −30°C months!

In the summer in Quebec, it's a produce free-for-all and an annual reminder of how lucky we are to live where we do. A combination of fresh blueberries, melons, corn, peas, tomatoes, and peaches all make appearances in our salads. And being located on the shores of the Saint Lawrence River means that spring brings a whole host of crabby, clammy, shrimpy, lobstery seafood goodness our way too.

# Your No-Fail Salad Equipment

A small blender for some of our favorite herby dressings

A salad spinner

Clean cutting board

A large bowl for tossing.

we suggest metal because you can bang them around without damaging, and they don't stain or retain flavors from previous marinades or salad mixes

A good knife

A squeeze bottle for dressing

Trusty tongs

# MAKING MANDY'S
# SALADS AT HOME

Many of our friends and guests—some of whom are great cooks—tell us they find making salads at home to be a drag. Too much chopping, salad spinning, and an almost innate inability to memorize any good dressing recipes. So we wanted to create this book to share our recipes and set you on a no-fail salad course for life! Trust us: the ingredients in our recipes are all very accessible, and the prep lists and steps of the methods are not at all overwhelming.

We've ordered the salads in this book roughly in the same order we developed them for our menu at Mandy's—there's no real rhyme or reason for where you should start, just dive in and enjoy! To get the most out of them, we suggest you start by making each salad as the recipe suggests, with the dressings (see page 11) and toppings we recommend. Once you've tried a few, you'll get the hang of things, and then you can mix and match each salad with almost any other dressing or topping you like. This works for our vegetarian or vegan readers, too—feel free to sub ingredients in and out as works for you. Get creative, and customize!

Unless otherwise specified, each of the salad recipes is for one person to enjoy but can easily be scaled up to feed more. Making your own salads is all about organization and habit. Plan ahead, and just one hour a week can yield three salad dressings (see page 11) and enough chopping that you'll have a different salad for every lunch that week! And that's your week sorted: simple and delicious.

And that was our aim for this book. Simple and delicious.

## NOTE ABOUT OUR DRESSINGS

Our salad dressings fit into two categories—dressings with fresh herbs and dressings without. Those with fresh herbs yield 1 cup of dressing and will be at their best for up to three days refrigerated. Those without fresh herbs make 2 cups and will last up to seven days refrigerated.

The idea behind the yield of these recipes is that there should be enough dressing for 5 to 6 salads, or a week's worth of lunches, with our 2-cup dressings. At Mandy's we provide ⅓ cup (80 ml) of dressing for a takeout salad, but a salad should always be dressed to one's personal preference.

## NOTE ON MEASUREMENTS

We all know that eating well—both health-wise and joy-wise—is all about eating real food and keeping it heavy on the veggies, e.g., salads. While developing and testing the recipes for this book, we realized very quickly that we didn't want to be weighing out lettuce leaves, or cherry tomatoes, or grated carrots for our salads and grain bowls. It started feeling like a diet book, which is not what a Mandy's salad is about. At all.

What we're talking about here is healthy, fun, plentiful, and best of all, full of FLAVORFUL ingredients.

So for the majority of our measurements, we use cups and tablespoons, a more casual alternative to weighted metric. That said, we're all about the ratios that lead to DELICIOUS, and so we have included metric measurements when it's important or might make things easier for you—including for our desserts, because well, baking is a whole other animal.

## NOTE ON INGREDIENTS

Like we said before, whenever possible we use local and organic ingredients and suggest you do too. As well, unless the recipe states otherwise, please assume:

- Eggs are large and freshly farmed;
- Herbs are fresh (and remember . . . cilantro and parsley stems have a ton of flavor, so never omit them!);
- Olive oil is extra virgin;
- Ginger is fresh.

# Chocolate Chip Cookies

We often leave work with well-intentioned cookies for our kids, but somehow they "disappear" before we get home!

MANDY | It began with chocolate chip cookies. I remember baking them after high school and laying them out on our family's JennAir stovetop vent to cool so they would be ready for us to gobble up even faster. One batch was adequate for three of my friends. Or for me, my brother, and my dad, with a 2-liter container of Québon milk. Then would come rolling out shortbread with my mom and Nana at Christmas time; then trying to master a flourless chocolate cake with salty caramel sauce and bringing it to every dinner party for months. But fast forward to 2020, and approximately 100,000 chocolate chip cookies are sold per year across Mandy's locations—they are our original and best-selling treat!

# NOTE ON NON-SALAD RECIPES

While we have always been pretty clear about our mission to be gourmet salad experts, we also listen to feedback and try to accommodate as many eaters out there as we can. So at Mandy's, and in this book, we've included a whole lot of other fun stuff.

Smoothies have been on the menu since day one, as for us the best way to start the day is with a blender full of fresh berries, a plant-based milk, spinach, and zesty ginger or fresh mint and basil. We've kept the best-selling ones (Tropical, Rise and Shine) on the menu and introduced some healthier options as well. Back in 2004, our brother Josh was the one standing on a Westmount street, with his good looks and killer smile, trying to lure people into Mandy's with smoothie samples set out on a little pastel Ikea kitchen tray.

> *Note: Throughout the smoothie section, we use "plant-based milk," which is your choice of soy, almond, oat, rice, hemp, cashew, coconut, etc. milk.*

Our grain bowls are an alternative to our green leafy salads where the "base" is a grain rather than lettuce—e.g., brown rice, quinoa, rice vermicelli—and then the usual suspects are added on top or mixed throughout. Grain bowls are also a fun winter option, as they can be served warm with our homemade dressings drizzled over top.

And of course we have sweets, because sweets are where it all began (see page 12)! Many of the recipes in the sweets chapter are for desserts Mandy makes at home that we're currently developing for our restaurants, and they are evocative of an old-school bake sale. While we don't see a Mandy's Bakery in our future necessarily, beware: these treats will go quickly!

# The Look of Mandy's

REBECCA | I think there's something luxurious about eating a salad out of a really gorgeous bowl with a gold-plated fork. Yes, we do quite simple food at Mandy's, but we make our resto environment feel pretty chic so the whole salad affair feels more . . . well, fancy. When you're at Mandy's, it's more than just eating a salad: it's an entire sensory experience. We take pride in bringing to our restaurants all the things that we love most. Whether it's a new album, recipe, or piece of decor, we want our guests to feel as if they were in an extension of our homes. And we're not minimalists! Mandy's is very much "more is more" as far as style—and salads—go.

Regardless of location, we have the same philosophy on the look and feel we want to create. Let's call it Rebecca's Rules. When creating a warm and inviting new space, here are some elements I always make sure to incorporate into the design:

*A gallery-style framed wall with family photos*

*Mixing old with new*

Large vintage-looking mirrors to create light and depth in the space

Always using inspiration from a recent travel trip; for example, our last visit to the Bahamas inspired new palm arrangements.

Lamps, sconces, or low-hanging dimmable lighting

Bright, colorful artwork

Vibrant, warm colors

Having an abundance of fresh flowers and greenery

MARBLE, MARBLE, MARBLE

A mix of patterns. More is more!

Old Montreal location

Sp COMMAND

POUR emp

PLEASE order HERE FOR

MANDY'S

Mango Magic (page 35), with chia seeds and hemp hearts

# Smoothies

CHAPTER ONE

# AMAZON
### Makes one 16-ounce smoothie

*Nut butter and chocolate is one of our favorite flavor combos (Reese's Pieces are a weak spot!), but for this recipe we opted for something a wee bit healthier (although not too much!) with almond butter, a plant-based milk, banana, and of course . . . Nutella.*

## INGREDIENTS

- ½ banana, broken into 3 to 4 pieces
- ¾ cup cold plant-based milk
- 3 tablespoons Nutella
- 2 tablespoons almond butter
- 1 teaspoon vanilla extract
- ½ cup ice cubes

## DIRECTIONS

Add the banana, plant-based milk, Nutella, almond butter, vanilla extract, and ice to your blender. Pulse for 5 to 8 seconds and then blend on medium for 20 to 30 seconds. Once smooth, pour into your smoothie cup and enjoy immediately.

# TROPICAL

*Makes one 16-ounce smoothie*

*Pineapples and mangos and coconuts—yes, please! Montreal may not have these ingredients locally (or the palm trees pictured on our restaurant wallpaper), but it sure feels like the real tropics here when the combined heat and humidity factor reaches 40°C in late July!*

## INGREDIENTS

- ½ banana, broken into 3 to 4 pieces
- 5 to 6 chunks fresh pineapple
- ¼ cup frozen mango cubes
- ¼ cup frozen strawberries
- ½ cup orange juice
- ½ cup coconut water
- ½ cup ice cubes

## DIRECTIONS

Add all of the fruit, the orange juice, the coconut water, and ice to your blender. Pulse for 5 to 8 seconds and then blend on medium for 20 to 30 seconds. Once smooth, pour into your smoothie cup and enjoy immediately.

# MONTREAL (MTL)
# PIÑA COLADA

*Makes one 16-ounce smoothie*

REBECCA | *One of my favorite decor items is fresh pineapple—the fresher, the better. But after its perfect ripeness begins to fade, what to do with all the sweet, juicy pineapples? Another delicious solution to reduce our waste . . . the Montreal (MTL) Piña Colada!*

## INGREDIENTS

- ½ banana, broken into 3 to 4 pieces
- 1 cup cold coconut milk
- 5 to 6 chunks fresh pineapple
- 2 tablespoons shredded coconut
- 4 mint leaves, torn
- ½ cup ice cubes

## DIRECTIONS

Add the banana, coconut milk, fresh pineapple, shredded coconut, mint, and ice to your blender. Pulse for 5 to 8 seconds and then blend on medium for 20 to 30 seconds. Once smooth, pour into your smoothie cup and enjoy immediately.

# RISE AND SHINE

*Makes one 16-ounce smoothie*

**The perfect smoothie after a summer morning run.**

## INGREDIENTS

- ½ banana, broken into 3 to 4 pieces
- 2 tablespoons almond butter
- ½ cup frozen blueberries
- 1 teaspoon flax seeds
- ¾ cup cold plant-based milk
- ½ cup ice cubes

## DIRECTIONS

Add the banana, almond butter, frozen blueberries, flax seeds, plant-based milk, and ice to your blender. Pulse for 5 to 8 seconds and then blend on medium for 20 to 30 seconds. Once smooth, pour into your smoothie cup and enjoy immediately.

# THE SHAKTI

*Makes one 16-ounce smoothie*

*Ed, our beloved general manager when we opened our Crescent Street location in 2015, is a vegan raw food master and is always bringing or making us the most vibrant concoctions. He's also very spiritual and taught us that the Hindu word Shakti means "the female principle of divine energy." If ever we were tired or pregnant or nursing or low on pretty much any kind of energy, he would throw all these ingredients together for us, and we appreciated every last ounce. It's pure life force and so vibrantly green, just looking at it makes you feel rejuvenated.*

NOTE: REFRIGERATE THE PINEAPPLE, GINGER, AND MINT FOR
AT LEAST ONE HOUR BEFORE MAKING THIS RECIPE.

## INGREDIENTS

- ½ banana, broken into 3 to 4 pieces
- 1 tablespoon maple syrup
- 5 to 6 chunks fresh pineapple
- 2 mint leaves, torn
- ½ avocado
- 1 teaspoon freshly grated or finely chopped ginger
- 1 cup shredded curly kale
- 1 cup baby spinach
- 1¼ cups apple cider

## DIRECTIONS

Add the banana, maple syrup, chilled pineapple, mint, avocado, ginger, kale, spinach, and apple cider to your blender. Pulse for 5 to 8 seconds and then blend on medium for 20 to 30 seconds. Once smooth, pour into your smoothie cup and enjoy immediately.

# PRETTY IN PINK

*Makes one 16-ounce smoothie*

*What better way to celebrate millennials' favorite color than with a smoothie called "Pretty in Pink"? It's got berries, zesty lime, some creamy almond milk, and our favorite—fresh basil leaves.*

## INGREDIENTS

- 1 whole banana, broken into smaller pieces
- ½ cup frozen strawberries
- ½ cup cold almond milk or other plant-based milk
- ½ cup apple cider
- 1 teaspoon lime juice
- 3 basil leaves

## DIRECTIONS

Add the banana, strawberries, almond milk, apple cider, lime juice, and basil to your blender. Pulse for 5 to 8 seconds and then blend on medium for 20 to 30 seconds. Once smooth, pour into your smoothie cup and enjoy immediately.

# DATE ME

### Makes one 16-ounce smoothie

Often, the name of a menu item starts as a joke behind closed doors, but some of them are just so funny or corny that they actually stick. This combination of dates, espresso, nut butter, and cacao is a great kick start to your morning (along with the Bulletproof Coffee, page 39) or that post-lunch slump.

## INGREDIENTS

- ¼ cup espresso
- 2 to 3 large Medjool dates, pitted
- 1 whole banana, broken into smaller pieces
- 3 tablespoons almond butter
- ¾ cup cold plant-based milk
- 1 teaspoon cacao powder
- 1 tablespoon hemp seeds

## DIRECTIONS

In a small bowl, pour the espresso over the dates to soften them as needed. Transfer to your blender and add the banana, almond butter, plant-based milk, cacao powder, and hemp seeds. Pulse for 5 to 8 seconds and then blend on medium for 20 to 30 seconds. Once smooth, pour into your smoothie cup and enjoy immediately.

# MANGO MAGIC

*Makes one 16-ounce smoothie*

*Do you want to consume superfoods in a delicious, cold, drinkable form? So do we! This silky orange blend highlights immunity-boosting turmeric, hydrating electrolytes from coconut, zippy stomach-soothing and circulatory help from freshly grated ginger, and all that vitamin C found in luscious mango.*

## INGREDIENTS

- 1 cup frozen mango cubes
- 1 teaspoon fresh grated or finely chopped ginger
- ½ teaspoon ground turmeric
- ½ cup cold coconut milk
- 1 cup apple cider
- 1 teaspoon lime juice

## DIRECTIONS

Add the mango, ginger, turmeric, coconut milk, apple cider, and lime juice to your blender. Pulse for 5 to 8 seconds and then blend on medium for 20 to 30 seconds. Once smooth, pour into your smoothie cup and enjoy immediately.

# BERRY AÇAÍ

*Makes one 16-ounce smoothie*

*Açaí—pronounced "ah-sigh-EE"—is the magical Brazilian super-fruit that boasts many health benefits, such as increasing your antioxidant levels to help neutralize damaging free radicals; boosting your energy level; supporting your immune system; and promoting a healthy gut.*

## INGREDIENTS

- 1 whole banana, broken into smaller pieces
- ½ cup frozen mango cubes
- ½ cup frozen strawberries
- ½ cup frozen blueberries
- ¼ cup açaí berries
- 1 tablespoon almond butter
- ¾ cup cold plant-based milk

## DIRECTIONS

Add the banana, mango, strawberries, blueberries, açaí, almond butter, and plant-based milk to your blender. Pulse for 5 to 8 seconds and then blend on medium for 20 to 30 seconds. Once smooth, pour into your smoothie cup and enjoy immediately.

# BULLETPROOF COFFEE

*Makes one 16-ounce smoothie*

The creator of Canada's Bulletproof diet, Dave Asprey, thought up the combination of butter, MCT (medium-chain triglycerides), and coffee when he was hiking in Tibet and needed a boost of energy. Fat keeps you fuller for longer, much more than sugary foods that tend to make your blood sugar spike and then crash. The idea that this combo "invigorates the mind and eradicates mental fog" is tried, tested, and true according to MMA fighters, chefs, nutritionists, and holistic and integrative medicine doctors.

NOTE: IT'S VERY IMPORTANT TO WHIP THIS SMOOTHIE UP IN A BLENDER TO MAKE IT VERY FROTHY. DO NOT JUST STIR IT VIGOROUSLY, OTHERWISE YOU'LL END UP DRINKING BLACK COFFEE WITH A POOL OF BUTTERY OIL ON TOP. EW.

## INGREDIENTS

- 2½ heaping tablespoons freshly ground coffee beans of your choice
- 1 tablespoon Brain Octane Oil or your preferred brand of MCT oil
- 1 to 2 tablespoons grass-fed, unsalted (very important) butter or 1 to 2 teaspoons of grass-fed ghee, organic if possible
- 1 teaspoon cinnamon (optional)
- 1 tablespoon manuka honey (optional) or your best-quality honey

## DIRECTIONS

Brew 1 cup of coffee using the ground coffee. Transfer to your blendar and add the Brain Octane Oil, butter or ghee, cinnamon and manuka honey. Blend on medium for 20 to 30 seconds until it looks like a creamy latte. There will be a good amount of foam on top. Pour into your smoothie cup and enjoy immediately.

Wolfe Salad (page 54)

# Salads

· CHAPTER TWO ·

# Shanghai Salad

◦ SERVES 1 ◦

We thought it only fitting to begin our first book with
our most popular salad: the Shanghai.

In the early 2000s, our family had an annual summer get-together with a
few other families at our cottage on a lake in the Laurentian mountains of
Quebec. One of the moms, Sandy Martz, would bring this killer salad with
toasted ramen noodles and a sweet sesame dressing that we couldn't get
enough of. We just *had* to know how to make it! She gladly shared, we tweaked
it a bit, and it has remained one of our top-selling salads ever since!

**NOTE: FOR A HIT OF PROTEIN, WE SUGGEST ADDING MOCK CHICKEN (PAGE 142).**

## INGREDIENTS

- ◦ 2 cups chopped romaine lettuce
- ◦ 2 cups mesclun greens
- ◦ ½ avocado, diced
- ◦ ¼ cup drained canned mandarin orange slices
- ◦ ¼ cup halved cherry tomatoes
- ◦ ¼ cup shredded carrot
- ◦ ½ cup Crispy Ramen Noodles (page 150)
- ◦ 2 tablespoons black and white sesame seeds

- ◦ ⅓ cup Sweet Sesame Dressing (page 156)

## DIRECTIONS

Combine all of the ingredients in a large stainless-steel bowl. Top with the dressing, and using tongs, toss until well mixed and dressed.

# Mexi Salad

∘ SERVES 1 ∘

Before we opened our first salad counter in 2004, Mandy was teaching ESL (English as a second language) in Toronto and had a myriad of Mexican and Central and South American students with whom she would also cook and partake in potluck dinners. Smoky cumin, lime juice, and zingy cilantro came to play a huge part in the weekly potluck menus, and so when Mandy's opened, one of the first salads we served was this mellow Mexi—perhaps more southern California than northern Mexico—complete with corn, black beans, tortilla chips, and diced tomatoes.

**NOTE: FOR SOMETHING MOREISH, ADD SOME ROASTED CHICKEN BREAST (PAGE 149).**

## INGREDIENTS

- 2 cups chopped romaine lettuce
- 2 cups mesclun greens
- ½ avocado, diced
- ¼ cherry tomatoes, halved
- ¼ cup shredded carrot (we know: not very "Mexi", but they look very pretty!) or diced orange bell pepper
- ¼ cup canned corn kernels, drained and rinsed
- ¼ cup canned black beans, drained and rinsed
- ½ cup tortilla chips (any plain salted version will do)
- 2 tablespoons torn cilantro leaves

- ⅓ cup Cilantro Cumin Dressing (page 162)

## DIRECTIONS

Combine all of the ingredients in a large stainless-steel bowl. Top with the dressing, and using tongs, toss until well mixed and dressed.

## La Belle Salad

◦ SERVES 1 ◦

MANDY | Previously known as the December Salad, this combination of sweet and salty ingredients was featured one December as the monthly salad, and it became wildly popular. Not only that, but my dear friend and co-parent Isabelle, known as Belle, would order it every single time she came in for a salad that month. Not sure where you are from, but over here in Montreal, "December" connotes a chilly feeling, whereas "Belle" is beautiful and appealing. So why not name the salad after its number-one customer and conjure up a little excitement? This salad is also one we point newcomers to, and it keeps guests coming back . . . See for yourself!

### INGREDIENTS

- ◦ 2 cups chopped romaine lettuce
- ◦ 2 cups mesclun greens
- ◦ ½ avocado, diced
- ◦ ¼ cup diced pear
- ◦ ¼ cup shredded carrot
- ◦ ¼ cup Parmesan flakes
- ◦ ½ cup Homemade Pita Chips (page 150)

- ◦ ⅓ cup Sweet Sesame Dressing (page 156)

### DIRECTIONS

Combine all of the ingredients in a large stainless-steel bowl. Top with the dressing, and using tongs, toss until well mixed and dressed.

# The Welcome Collective

*Becca with her daughter, Coco, and our friend Thompson, one of the first refugee claimants we met in 2017*

In November 2017, we answered a call to help refugee claimants find homes in Quebec. Our goal for the Christmas 2017 season was to furnish the homes and cover the basic needs of 30 refugee claimant families. For a few months, along with our husbands and dear friends, we abandoned our jobs and our own families to heed the call of others in need. It is hard to put into words the profound impact this experience had on us, but if we had to summarize it would be something like this: "when you have more than you need, you build a longer table, not a higher fence."

Leveraging our social media platforms, we reached out to our networks and were quickly overwhelmed and humbled by the outpouring of help and donations that came our way. Our restaurants became drop-off points for used clothing and furnishings for families in need. In the end, we managed to move 200 families and furnish 200 apartments! In the years since we have wanted to keep helping, so in 2019 we established the Welcome Collective and obtained charitable status. We now have eight board members, and a staff of about ten lovely individuals coordinating the drop-offs of basic essentials for refugee claimant families leaving shelters and venturing out into their own unfurnished apartments.

And we bring it back to salads to make this all go 'round. Now one dollar from every monthly special salad sold (every day/all year long) goes to the Welcome Collective. The money donated helps to pay for moving trucks, and the rent for a warehouse to store all the donated items, among many other things.

We have now met so many beautiful people from around the world who have been subject to such hardships. What this has done for our appreciation and gratitude for our own circumstances is immeasurable. Thank you so much to Noelle Sorbara and the entire WeCo family. This has been the most meaningful work we have ever done, and you continue to teach us that the heart knows no bounds.

# Tokyo Salad

◦ SERVES 1 ◦

REBECCA | When we think of Japanese food, we think simplicity, elegance, purity . . . This is a vegan salad that features one of our best-selling dressings, full of that coveted umami. The ingredients are all raw, save for the miso-citrus–marinated tofu, and the dressing is a nutty tamari-garlic party in your mouth. Fun fact: this is one of my favorite salads, and I usually add diced red onions for extra crunch and punch. I suggest you do the same!

## INGREDIENTS

- 2 cups chopped romaine lettuce
- 2 cups mesclun greens
- ¼ cup shredded carrot
- ¼ cup shredded red cabbage
- ¼ cup small broccoli florets
- ¼ cup diced cucumber
- ½ cup Roasted Marinated Tofu (page 148)
- 2 tablespoons black and white sesame seeds
- 2 tablespoons diced red onion (optional)

- ⅓ cup Tamari Dressing (page 155)

## DIRECTIONS

Combine all of the ingredients in a large stainless-steel bowl. Top with the dressing, and using tongs, toss until well mixed and dressed.

# R&D Extraordinaire Salad

◦ SERVES 1 ◦

We know, we know, what a name! Back in our early days when we only hired young hardworking women (i.e., mostly our friends), we had two special ladies working for us: Raegan Steinberg and Danielle Samuelson (Raegan now owns and operates Arthur's Nosh Bar here in Montreal with her husband, and chef, Alex Cohen; Danielle built her life in New York City, and is still a *gourmande* at heart). Every single day they worked in our kitchen, they would make this combo of ingredients for lunch, and somehow they never got tired of it! It became so popular that we said, "All right, it's going on the menu!" Salty Parmesan shavings, creamy avocado, sweet, tart strawberries, crunchy pita chips, some fresh veggies, and a classic balsamic dressing—voilà!

## INGREDIENTS

- 2 cups chopped romaine lettuce
- 2 cups mesclun greens
- ½ avocado, diced
- ¼ cup diced cucumber
- ¼ cup shredded carrot
- ¼ cup sliced strawberries
- ¼ cup Parmesan flakes
- ½ cup Homemade Pita Chips (page 150)

- ⅓ cup Classic Balsamic Dressing (page 166)

## DIRECTIONS

Combine all of the ingredients in a large stainless-steel bowl. Top with the dressing, and using tongs, toss until well mixed and dressed.

# The Fave

◦ SERVES 1 ◦

We have been through many phases of food cravings and salad creations—
one of which was our obsession with all things honey-mustard: the pairing
of sweet floral honey with the deep kick of a great mustard. We were used to
having it served over brisket at Jewish High Holidays or slathered on some rye
bread in a deli turkey sandwich. But we needed some healthy sides to go with
it, so we added some broccoli, corn, carrots, and avocado, crispy pita chips,
and some slices of deli turkey. All of a sudden, it was our fave go-to salad.

## INGREDIENTS

- 3 cups chopped romaine lettuce
- 1 cup arugula
- ½ avocado, diced
- ¼ cup small broccoli florets (raw)
- ¼ cup canned corn kernels, drained and rinsed
- ¼ cup shredded carrot
- ¼ cup Parmesan flakes
- ½ cup Homemade Pita Chips (page 150)
- 2 tablespoons raw sunflower seeds

- ⅓ cup Honey Mustard Dressing (page 170)

## DIRECTIONS

Combine all of the ingredients in a large stainless-steel bowl. Top with the dressing, and using tongs, toss until well mixed and dressed.

## ◦ SERVES 1 ◦

MANDY | The great thing about being in a kitchen with a prep line of about 60 containers of cleaned, chopped, marinated, and ready-to-serve ingredients is that at any given time I get to play with the combo of ingredients and switch up my "flavor of the month," so to speak. Enter the Wolfe Salad: a salad with a grainy undertone (predating any of our grain bowls) that was an instant favorite of both our parents, Judy and Jason, and quickly became a fave of our staff and our guests. After the almighty Shanghai and the epic Chocolate Chip Cookie, the WoBo (as it's affectionately nicknamed) reigns supreme. Moreish and filling, it's still a dinner staple in our house.

## INGREDIENTS

- ◦ 2 cups mesclun greens
- ◦ 1 cup arugula
- ◦ 1 cup shredded curly kale
- ◦ ½ avocado, diced
- ◦ ¼ cup shredded carrot
- ◦ ¼ cup cherry tomatoes, halved
- ◦ ½ cup Quinoa (page 201)
- ◦ ¼ cup Parmesan flakes
- ◦ 2 tablespoons roasted walnut pieces
- ◦ 2 tablespoons black and white sesame seeds

- ◦ ⅓ cup Tamari Dressing (page 155)

## DIRECTIONS

Combine all of the ingredients in a large stainless-steel bowl. Top with the dressing, and using tongs, toss until well mixed and dressed.

# Lumberjack Salad

∘ SERVES 1 ∘

A salad fit for your inner *coureur des bois*.

When we set up our first shop in the back of Mimi & Coco, female customers were obviously very much in their element, trying on designer Italian pointelle camisoles and . . . buying salads. Their male partners were awkwardly standing around, waiting for them, so we came up with a salad that really needed no further enticing or explaining. We tried to think of the most "hungry carnivore man" ingredients for a salad (think heaping bacon, turkey, chicken, cheese, pita, etc.) and actually even called it the "Man Salad" for a time, until common sense got the better of us.

This salad is for the *very* hungry. Plaid flannel not included.

## INGREDIENTS

- 4 cups chopped romaine lettuce
- ½ avocado, diced
- ¼ cup cherry tomatoes, halved
- ¼ cup sliced white mushroom caps
- ¼ cup Roasted Chicken Breast (page 149)
- 2 slices bacon, cut into pieces and fried until crispy
- ¼ cup chopped sliced turkey
- ¼ cup shredded mozzarella
- ¼ cup sliced scallion (green part only)
- ½ cup Homemade Pita Chips (page 150)

- ⅓ cup Caesar Dressing (page 156)

## DIRECTIONS

Combine all of the ingredients in a large stainless-steel bowl. Top with the dressing, and using tongs, toss until well mixed and dressed.

# Mediterranean Salmon

◦ SERVES 1 ◦

MANDY | At a certain point the menu at Mandy's was skewing heavily toward sesame/miso/tamari everrrrrrrything (another one of my food phases), and we wanted to take the spotlight off my obsession with Southeast Asia and bring the salads back to more versatile and varied flavor sources. Hence this more Mediterranean savory salmon, marinated and basted with briny capers, tart lemons, sticky concentrated sun-dried tomatoes, and heaps of dill, garlic, and onions. I think my favorite toasted nut is the beautiful pine nut (especially for salad), and what better pairing with these flavors than fresh basil, salty chunks of feta, creamy avocado, and mounds of perfectly roasted flaked salmon on top?

## INGREDIENTS

- 2 cups baby spinach
- 1 cup mesclun greens
- 1 cup shredded curly kale
- ½ avocado, diced
- 2 tablespoons sliced scallion (green part only)
- ¼ cup diced red bell pepper
- ¼ cup cubed feta
- 2 tablespoons toasted pine nuts
- 1 tablespoon torn basil leaves
- 1 tablespoon torn mint leaves
- 1 tablespoon dill fronds
- ¼ pound Roasted Mediterranean Salmon (page 144), skin off

- ⅓ cup Wild Goddess Dressing (page 158)

## DIRECTIONS

Combine all of the ingredients, except for the salmon, in a large stainless-steel bowl. Top with the dressing, and using tongs, toss until well mixed and dressed. Transfer to a serving bowl and arrange the salmon, broken into large flaky pieces, over top.

Atwater location

# Habibi Salad

◦ SERVES 1 ◦

MANDY | One of our favorite cuisines is Middle Eastern, and Lebanese in particular, as my husband, Mike Zaidan, was born in Beirut. *Habibi* ("my love") was one of the first words I learned and is such a cherished pet name for any loved one, why not give a salad that kind of love too? Chock full of salty feta, tomatoes, cucumbers, fresh mint and parsley, and legumes like chickpeas and lentils, all served up with a tahini-lemon dressing spiked with a vibrant healthy yellow turmeric boost. *Sahtein*, habibis and habibtis!

## INGREDIENTS

- 2 cups chopped romaine lettuce
- 2 cups mesclun greens
- ½ cup Quinoa (page 201)
- ¼ cup canned chickpeas, drained and rinsed
- ¼ cup canned lentils, drained and rinsed
- ¼ cup diced cucumber
- ¼ cup cherry tomatoes, halved
- ⅛ red onion, sliced paper thin
- ¼ cup cubed feta
- ¼ cup Roasted Sweet Potato (page 146)
- 2 tablespoons torn mint leaves
- 2 tablespoons chopped flat-leaf parsley leaves

- ⅓ cup Turmeric Tahini Dressing (page 157)

## DIRECTIONS

Combine all of the ingredients in a large stainless-steel bowl. Top with the dressing, and using tongs, toss until well mixed and dressed.

*Mandy and her habibi, in Italy*

# Endless Summer Salad

◦ SERVES 1 ◦

The first summer we were open in our Crescent Street location (2015), we were concocting a monthly special for July. It was a spectacular month, and we were so busy—those sunny summer months are such a cherished and joyful time in Montreal with patios packed and everyone out basking in the heat. This salad was a real hit from day one, and like so many monthly specials that hit it out of the park, we kept it. However, we changed its name to hold on to that special feeling only Montreal summers can elicit . . .

## INGREDIENTS

- 2 cups chopped romaine lettuce
- 1 cup mesclun greens
- 1½ cups shredded curly kale
- ½ avocado, diced
- ½ cup Roasted Marinated Tempeh (page 143)
- ¼ cup shredded carrot
- ¼ cup diced red bell pepper
- ¼ cup pomegranate seeds
- ½ Ataulfo mango, diced (optional)
- 2 tablespoons Crispy Fried Shallots (page 151)
- 2 tablespoons pumpkin seeds
- 2 tablespoons basil leaves
- 2 tablespoons torn cilantro leaves

- ⅓ cup Endless Summer Dressing (page 166)

## DIRECTIONS

Combine all of the ingredients in a large stainless-steel bowl. Top with the dressing, and using tongs, toss until well mixed and dressed.

# Superfood Salad

◦ SERVES 1 ◦

Every January, with the best of intentions for the new year ahead of us, we aim to feature a monthly salad geared toward everyone's resolutions to take better care of themselves and eat healthy. This salad is the amalgamation of popular superfoods claiming to lengthen your life, boost your immunity, detoxify your liver, tighten your skin, and reverse aging (okay, maybe not that one, but you never know!). Plus, it's super pretty to look at and hits all the spots for crunchy, tangy, salty, sweet, and mighty colorful.

## INGREDIENTS

- 2 cups baby spinach
- 1 cup shredded curly kale
- 1 cup arugula
- ½ avocado, diced
- ½ cup Quinoa (page 201)
- ¼ cup diced apple
- ¼ cup halved cherry tomatoes
- ¼ cup small broccoli florets (raw)
- ¼ cup Roasted Sweet Potato (page 146)
- 2 tablespoons pomegranate seeds
- 2 tablespoons torn mint leaves
- 2 tablespoons chopped flat-leaf parsley leaves

- ⅓ cup Mandy's House Dressing (page 155)

## DIRECTIONS

Combine all of the ingredients in a large stainless-steel bowl. Top with the dressing, and using tongs, toss until well mixed and dressed.

# Lobster Salad

◦ SERVES 1 ◦

Every year, from the time we were born, at the end of every summer, our parents drove the family down to the Maine coast to Kennebunkport for a whole week before school started back up. This was the only time we ever ate lobster, and boy oh boy, did we ever learn to love, appreciate, and look forward to eating Maine lobster. Not only is it one of the tastiest, most delicately sweet and salty shellfish, but lobster is a meal that conjures up some of the happiest of memories of times spent with our other two siblings, Jessie and Josh, as well as our late father, Jason. At Mandy's, we only feature lobster when it's in full season from June until September, to create the same anticipation that we felt growing up for that summer lobster love.

## INGREDIENTS

- ¼ pound cooked lobster meat
- 2 tablespoons melted unsalted butter
- 1 clove garlic, smashed
- 2 cups chopped romaine lettuce
- 2 cups mesclun greens
- ½ avocado, diced
- ¼ cup sliced cucumber
- 2 tablespoons sliced scallion (green part only)
- 2 tablespoons thinly sliced purple cabbage
- 2 tablespoons (thawed and rinsed) frozen edamame (optional)
- 2 tablespoons Crispy Fried Shallots (page 151)
- 2 tablespoons black and white sesame seeds

- ⅓ cup Sweet Miso Ginger Dressing (page 160)

## DIRECTIONS

In a large stainless-steel bowl, use your hands to break the lobster into bite-size pieces. Toss the lobster with the melted butter and the smashed garlic. Add the remaining ingredients to the bowl. Top with the dressing, and using tongs, toss until well mixed and dressed.

# Fancy Pants Niçoise Salad

◦ SERVES 1 OR 4 ◦

How many times have we been invited to a chic brunch or fancy lunch somewhere and been served a quiche and a side salad, along with some sort of sad, tepid salmon? So this salad is our Mandy's fix. We love a hybrid salad that incorporates eggs, potatoes, roasted salmon, punchy capers, sun-dried tomatoes, and French *haricots verts*, blanched to crunchy perfection and perfect for lunch or brunch.

## INGREDIENTS

- 2 tablespoons olive oil
- ¼ cup drained capers, patted dry
- 4 baby potatoes
- 2 cups thin green beans, trimmed
- 4 large eggs, at room temperature
- 1-pound organic salmon fillet (we use Atlantic), skin on
- Fine sea salt and freshly ground black pepper
- 4 cups frisée lettuce or mâche
- ¼ cup Niçoise olives, pitted
- ¼ cup sundried tomatoes in oil, drained and thinly sliced
- 1 tablespoon chopped fresh dill fronds

- ¼ cup Provençale Vinaigrette Dressing (page 160)

## DIRECTIONS

Heat the olive oil in a small saucepan over medium-high heat. Add the capers and cook, swirling the pan occasionally, until the capers burst and crisp, about 5 minutes. Transfer the capers to paper towels to drain. Let the oil cool and reserve it to rub on the salmon before cooking it.

Place the potatoes in a small saucepan and cover with cold water by 1 inch. Salt the water generously and bring to a boil, and cook potatoes until fork-tender, 15 to 20 minutes. Drain the potatoes, transfer to a plate, and set aside to cool.

Cook the green beans in the same saucepan with salted water until crisp-tender (the salt not only flavors your vegetables, but will help greens retain their vibrant color), about 2 minutes. Using a slotted spoon, transfer the beans to a bowl of ice water. Chill until cold, about 2 minutes. Transfer to paper towels and pat dry.

Place the eggs in the saucepan and bring the water to a rolling boil. Remove from heat and let sit with the lid on for 8 to 10 minutes, then transfer the eggs to a bowl of ice water and chill until cold, about 5 minutes. Peel and set aside.

Preheat the oven to 425°F.

Place the salmon on a parchment-lined sheet tray and rub the fish with the reserved caper oil. Season generously with salt and pepper. Roast until medium-rare (the salmon will be slightly translucent in the center), 12–15 minutes. If you like a more golden top, switch the oven to broil for the last 3 minutes. Once cooked to your liking, set aside to cool.

NOTE: THIS IS BEST PREPARED FOR A GROUP BECAUSE IF YOU'RE PREPPING THE INGREDIENTS INDIVIDUALLY, YOU MIGHT AS WELL PRODUCE THEM IN VOLUME: ARE YOU GOING TO WANT TO BOIL ONLY ONE BABY POTATO? NO. OR ONE EGG? OR TURN THE OVEN ON FOR A QUARTER-POUND OF SALMON? SAME THING.

SO THIS SALAD SERVES FOUR PEOPLE (BUT WE INCLUDE PLATING INSTRUCTIONS FOR ONE PERSON). ALSO, THIS IS A ROOM-TEMPERATURE SALAD, NOT A COLD-FROM-THE-FRIDGE SALAD. THEREFORE, IT'S BEST SERVED RIGHT AFTER YOU'VE FINISHED PREPPING ALL OF THE INGREDIENTS.

## TO SERVE THIS SALAD FOR 1 PERSON

On a plate, arrange 1 cup lettuce, followed by 1 baby potato, sliced; 1 hard-boiled egg, halved; ½ cup green beans; 1 tablespoon olives; 1 tablespoon sun-dried tomato slices; and a quarter of the cooked salmon (skin removed and discarded), flaked. Sprinkle with a generous amount of Maldon salt and a good grind of pepper and drizzle the Provençale dressing (including lemon segments) over top. Top with a quarter of the fried capers and a sprinkle of fresh dill.

## TO SERVE THIS SALAD FOR 4 PEOPLE

On a large platter, arrange a bed of lettuce, then top with the potatoes, halved eggs, green beans, olives, sun-dried tomatoes and the salmon (skin removed and discarded), flaked. Sprinkle with a generous amount of Maldon salt and a good grind of pepper and drizzle the Provençale dressing (including lemon segments) over top. Top with the fried capers and fresh dill.

° SERVES 1 °

The end of summer is a time of harvest, and in our minds, there are specific herbs that conjure up a feeling—crunchy rainbow-colored leaves on Montreal sidewalks, Canadian Thanksgiving feasts, the smell of sage and rosemary wafting from the family oven. So we came up with a sage-inspired dressing to accompany a mix of roasted sweet potatoes, toasted pecans, earthy floral pears from fall's harvest, and tangy goat cheese. It's a lovely side to a turkey- or poultry-based dinner or lunch and an absolute crowd pleaser.

**NOTE: TO UP THE ANTE ON THIS SALAD, WE SUGGEST ADDING SOME ROASTED SHREDDED HOISIN DUCK (PAGE 98).**

## INGREDIENTS

- 4 cups mesclun greens
- ¼ cup cubed Roasted Sweet Potatoes (page 146)
- ¼ cup diced pear
- ¼ cup crumbled goat cheese
- 2 tablespoons Crispy Fried Shallots (page 151)
- 2 tablespoons diced dried figs
- 2 tablespoons roasted pecan halves
- 2 tablespoons pumpkin seeds
- ¼ pound (1 cup) Roasted Shredded Hoisin Duck (page 98) (optional)

- ⅓ cup Wild Sage Dressing (page 161)

## DIRECTIONS

Combine all of the ingredients in a large stainless-steel bowl. Top with the dressing, and using tongs, toss until well mixed and dressed.

# Waldorf Salad

° SERVES 1 °

We created this very simple, whip-it-up-in-three-minutes version of the classic salad. If you love blue cheese and toasted walnuts with a little dried fruit, you're going to love our simple take on a Waldorf salad. Like all salads in this book, this one doubles easily if you're having someone over for lunch.

NOTE: WE'RE HUGE FANS OF BLUE CHEESE—THE STINKIER, THE BETTER!
HOWEVER, WE REALIZE NOT EVERYONE IS LIKE US, SO THIS SALAD CALLS FOR A MILDER
DANISH BLUE CHEESE, ALLOWING YOU TO STILL TAKE A WALK ON THE WALDORF SIDE.

## INGREDIENTS

- 2 cups mesclun greens
- 2 cups baby spinach
- ½ Honeycrisp apple, diced
- ½ Bartlett pear, diced
- ¼ cup crumbled Danish blue cheese
- ¼ cup toasted walnuts
- 2 tablespoons dried cranberries
- 2 tablespoons Crispy Fried Shallots (page 151)
- 1 teaspoon minced rosemary

- ⅓ cup Classic Balsamic Dressing (page 166)

## DIRECTIONS

Combine all of the ingredients in a large stainless-steel bowl. Top with the dressing, and using tongs, toss until well mixed and dressed.

Laurier location

# Deluxe Waldorf Salad

◦ SERVES 1 ◦

This salad was first featured in March 2019, when we had long removed the Waldorf salad from the menu, but still wanted to reintroduce some of its familiar flavors . . . with a makeover. We adore California champagne vinegar, pungent Gorgonzola, and zesty grated horseradish—all of these bold and subtle upgrades were part of the "deluxing" of the Waldorf.

## INGREDIENTS

- 1 cup mesclun greens
- ½ cup shredded curly kale
- ½ cup baby spinach
- ¼ cup chopped radicchio
- ½ Cortland apple, diced
- ¼ cup crumbled Gorgonzola
- ¼ cup toasted walnuts
- 1 tablespoon dried cranberries
- 1 tablespoon thinly sliced red onion
- 1 tablespoon freshly grated horseradish as garnish (optional)

- ⅓ cup Champagne Vinaigrette Dressing (page 161)

## DIRECTIONS

Combine all of the ingredients in a large stainless-steel bowl. Top with the dressing, and using tongs, toss until well mixed and dressed.

# Curry Quinoa Salad

◦ SERVES 1 ◦

MANDY | Judy Wolfe, aka Mom, used to make us this fabulous chicken salad (with a ton of Indian curry paste, mayonnaise, chopped fruit, and crunchy celery) to go in our sandwiches. The memory of it has never left me—I would crave the flavor of this curried chicken salad and think about how we could turn it into a proper, actual salad, and without any chicken in it. We've figured it out! There's something so delightful about the marriage of unusual ingredients, like celery, cashews, grapes, yogurt, and curry, but so satisfying when it hits the spot. Quinoa is definitely the healthier option, but this salad works equally well with couscous.

## INGREDIENTS

- 2 cups chopped romaine lettuce
- 2 cups mesclun greens
- ½ cup Quinoa (page 201)
- ¼ cup grated carrots
- ¼ cup halved red seedless grapes
- ¼ cup canned chickpeas, drained and rinsed
- 2 tablespoons diced celery
- 2 tablespoons diced red bell pepper
- 2 tablespoons diced pineapple (optional)
- 2 tablespoons roasted salted cashews
- 2 tablespoons torn cilantro leaves

- ⅓ cup Curried Yogurt Dressing (page 170)

## DIRECTIONS

Combine all of the ingredients in a large stainless-steel bowl. Top with the dressing, and using tongs, toss until well mixed and dressed.

Positano, 2001

# Roma Salad

◦ SERVES 1 ◦

REBECCA | So many Italian-inspired salads have pesto in their dressing or some variation on a red wine vinaigrette . . . Ain't nothin' wrong with either of those things, but we wanted to bring in the Italian sun and Italian cuisine's deep love of tomatoes. My husband, Vince, and I took a trip to the Amalfi coast when we first started dating, and it was also there that we got engaged in the summer of 2008. This salad is a marriage of unusual sweet and salty ingredients like figs with olives, and creamy bocconcini cheese with fresh basil leaves, served with sun-dried tomato dressing. Tastes like *la dolce vita* . . .

## INGREDIENTS

- 2 cups chopped romaine lettuce
- 2 cups mesclun greens
- ¼ cup small broccoli florets (raw)
- ⅛ red onion, sliced paper thin
- 2 tablespoons halved Kalamata olives
- 2 tablespoons torn basil leaves
- 2 tablespoons diced dried figs
- ¼ cup cubed bocconcini
- ½ cup toasted pine nuts (optional)

- ⅓ cup Sun-Dried Tomato Dressing (page 165)

## DIRECTIONS

Combine all of the ingredients in a large stainless-steel bowl. Top with the dressing, and using tongs, toss until well mixed and dressed.

# Kale Caesar Salad

∘ SERVES 1 ∘

When we created the first ever Mandy's menu, we were reaching far and
wide with globally inspired flavors. We asked a few of our friends and family
what they thought of the menu and they said, "Where's the Caesar salad?"
We were like, "Really, Caesar is what you want . . .?!" But we listened and
made an especially good one, with a healthy twist thanks to the kale.

## INGREDIENTS

- 3 cups chopped romaine lettuce
- 1 cup shredded lacinato kale
- ¼ cup shredded mozzarella
- ¼ cup Parmesan flakes
- 2 slices bacon, cut into
  pieces and fried until crispy
- 2 tablespoons capers, fried
  in 1 tablespoon of olive oil
  until they burst and crisp
- ½ cup Homemade Pita
  Chips (page 150)
- 1 hard-boiled Jammy Egg
  (page 148), sliced in half
  and then dusted with freshly
  ground black pepper

- ⅓ cup Caesar Dressing
  (page 156)

## DIRECTIONS

Combine all of the ingredients in a large stainless-steel bowl.
Top with the dressing, and using tongs, toss until well mixed
and dressed.

# Cobb Salad

◦ SERVES 1 ◦

So many stories are told about the origin of the "real" Cobb salad: was it Hollywood Brown Derby's owner Robert Howard Cobb or his chef that came up with the recipe? Something about it being very late at night and they only had leftovers to work with . . . In any case, necessity is the mother of invention, and we love all the classic ingredients used, like bacon and eggs. But as with all classics, we love to put our spin on things and freshen it up, in this case with a ton of green herbs in our Green Goddess dressing. Late-night salad, served all day long!

## INGREDIENTS

- 2 cups chopped romaine lettuce
- 2 cups mesclun greens
- ¼ cup halved cherry tomatoes
- 2 slices bacon, cut into pieces and fried until crispy
- ¼ cup sliced white mushroom caps
- ¼ cup sliced canned hearts of palm
- ¼ cup sliced scallion (green part only)
- ½ cup Homemade Pita Chips (page 150)
- 1 Jammy Egg (page 148), halved
- Fine sea salt
- Freshly ground black pepper

- ⅓ cup Green Goddess Dressing (page 158)

## DIRECTIONS

Combine all of the ingredients except the egg in a large stainless-steel bowl. Top with the dressing, and using tongs, toss until well mixed and dressed. Transfer to a serving bowl and top with the egg halves. Season generously with salt and pepper.

# Sopranos Salad

◦ SERVES 1 ◦

One of the integral ingredients that makes the whole of Montreal so damn delicious is our Italian community. From coffee at Caffè Italia to the cannoli at Alati-Caserta to the "Milano Special" sandwich at Café Milano in Saint-Léonard, what can we say? *Bro, it's the best.*

This salad is Saint Leo meets New Jersey meets Laurier Street in salad form. Here, instead of asking ourselves, "What would Tony do?" we wondered, "What would Tony make?" And because standing at the open refrigerator and snacking on deli meat isn't a recipe per se, we created this salad in honor of Tony Soprano's memory.

## INGREDIENTS

- 2 cups shredded iceberg lettuce
- 2 cups mixed greens
- ¼ cup loosely packed basil leaves, torn
- ¼ cup coarsely chopped radicchio
- ¼ cup pickled banana pepper rings
- 1 thin slice red onion
- 7 pitted Kalamata olives
- 7 cherry tomatoes, halved
- ⅓ cup coarsely chopped bocconcini
- ⅓ cup diced capocollo sausage
- 10 ruffled potato chips

- ⅓ cup Red Wine Vinny (or Vinnie) Dressing (page 163)

## DIRECTIONS

Combine all of the ingredients in a large stainless-steel bowl. Top with the dressing, and using tongs, toss until well mixed and dressed. Bada-bing!

# Mint Madness Salad

◦ SERVES 1 ◦

MANDY | While we were working on this book, we found some of our old "vintage" menus from about 10 years ago. These were printed on flimsy ream paper, then laminated at Bureau en Gros (Quebec's equivalent of Staples). And one of the salads we had back then was called Mint Madness! I have always been obsessed with fresh herbs. Each one has a story to tell and a menu you can create around it. Or, in our case, a salad. This beauty of a recipe has been on and off our menu for years, in various incarnations. We love pairing mint with the delicate anise flavor of fennel, and with pear, and salty hardened feta. It's a joy to play around with the subtlety versus dominance of certain ingredients—grapefruit is an amazing addition, as is watermelon in the peak of summer—and then infuse it all with the highlighted herb, in this case mint.

**NOTE: THIS SUMMERTIME SALAD IS PERFECT WITH THE ADDITION OF MOCK CHICKEN (PAGE 142) OR ROASTED CHICKEN BREAST (PAGE 149).**

## INGREDIENTS

- 1 cup chopped romaine lettuce
- 1 cup baby spinach
- 1 cup mesclun greens
- ½ pear, diced
- ½ avocado, diced
- ¼ cup shredded carrot
- ¼ fennel bulb, sliced thin with a mandoline
- ¼ cup chopped cucumber
- 2 tablespoons sliced thin red onion
- ¼ cup cubed feta
- 2 tablespoons toasted sunflower seeds
- 2 tablespoons torn mint leaves

- ⅓ cup Mint Madness Dressing (page 166)

## DIRECTIONS

Combine all of the ingredients in a large stainless-steel bowl. Top with the dressing, and using tongs, toss until well mixed and dressed.

# Hoisin Duck Salad

∘ SERVES 1 ∘

MANDY | One year, for my birthday, I ate out at a modern Peruvian place, Montreal's Tiradito restaurant, and one of the small plates was these little steamed buns with shredded duck and a ton of fresh cilantro, pickled onion, and crushed peanuts. So delicious. I was so haunted by their flavor that we did what we do best and turned it into a salad!

## INGREDIENTS

- 2 Bao Buns (page 101)
- ¼ pound (1 cup) Roasted Shredded Hoisin Duck (page 98)
- 2 cups shredded curly kale
- 1 cup arugula
- ½ cup "super slaw" (see Note)
- ¼ cup shredded carrot
- 2 tablespoons Pickled Red Onion (page 99)
- 2 tablespoons torn cilantro leaves
- 2 tablespoons black and white sesame seeds
- 1 tablespoon roasted peanuts

- ⅓ cup (80 ml) Hoisin Dressing (page 164)

## NOTES

This is, without a doubt, the most involved salad in this book as far as preparation goes. But it's also perhaps the most satisfying and sumptuous. This recipe has many moving parts, but each can be made on its own—the duck, the bao buns, the salad, or hoisin dressing—but the entire recipe, the sum of its parts, is when this salad sings: a great combination of sweet, salty, and earthy.

- Before you can assemble this salad in a bowl and devour it, you need to prepare the duck meat, which will need about four hours of cooking/resting time, as well as bao buns which can be made well ahead of time and frozen until ready to use.
- We added the buns to the salad to tempt you into turning your salad into a little sandwich! They are so worth making as a big batch.
- The duck meat provides enough for four portions of salad. If you wish to make a salad that serves four people, simply quadruple the ingredients for the kale, arugula, carrot, cilantro, sesame seeds, and peanuts.
- The "super slaw" can be found in the prepackaged salad section of any grocery store and generally consists of a combination of shredded kale, Brussels sprouts, red cabbage, and/or zucchini.

## DIRECTIONS

Warm up the bao buns and the duck meat as needed. In a large bowl, layer the kale, arugula, super slaw, and carrot, followed by the warm duck meat. Drizzle the dressing over top. Then garnish with the pickled onion, cilantro, sesame seeds, and roasted peanuts and top with the warm steamed buns.

# ROASTED SHREDDED HOISIN DUCK

## SERVES 4

The duck for this salad is roasted and pulled and then cooked in a hoisin and orange juice marinade, which results in a sweet, salty barbecued duck.

## INGREDIENTS

- One 4½ pound fresh duck
- Fine sea salt and freshly ground black pepper
- 1½ cups Hoisin Marinade (page 99)

## DIRECTIONS

Preheat the oven to 325°F.

Remove any giblets and the neck from the cavity and discard or reserve them for another use.

Lay the duck on a rack inside a roasting pan, breast side up. Season generously with salt and pepper. Slow-roast for 2 hours.

Remove the duck from the oven and use the point of a sharp knife to prick holes in the skin surrounding the breasts and thighs. Return to the oven and cook for another 1 hour and 15 minutes.

Carefully remove the roasting pan from the oven (it will contain a significant amount of melted duck fat). Transfer the duck to a cutting board and let it rest for 30 minutes. In the meantime, strain the hot fat and juices into a heatproof container. Let the juices cool completely and then transfer the fat (which will have risen to the top) to a different container and refrigerate it. It is especially excellent for pan-frying or roasting potatoes, and will keep for weeks in the fridge.

While the duck is cooling, make the Hoisin Marinade.

Use your hands to pull the duck apart into smaller pieces. The breasts should lift easily off the rib cage. Remove and discard the skin, and working over a bowl, pull off and reserve all of the duck meat. Use 2 forks or your hands to pull the meat into smaller bite-size shredded pieces.

Pour 1½ cups of the Hoisin Marinade (reserve the leftover marinade for the Hoisin Dressing (page 164)) into the bowl containing the duck meat and stir until well combined. If you are not planning to make the salad right away, refrigerate the marinating meat until ready to use, up to 24 hours ahead.

Preheat the oven to 450°F.

Spread the marinated duck meat out on a large sheet tray. Roast it for 10 minutes or until the duck pieces start to caramelize around the edges. Keep the meat warm while you start building the salad (refrigerate any portion of the duck you are not using for up to 3 days).

# HOISIN MARINADE

MAKES 1⅔ CUPS (400 ML)

## INGREDIENTS

- 1 cup hoisin sauce
- ¼ cup orange juice
- 5 cloves garlic
- 2 tablespoons coarsely chopped ginger
- 2 tablespoons rice vinegar

## DIRECTIONS

In a blender, combine all of the ingredients. Process on medium-high speed for 10 to 15 seconds—it's okay if there are still pieces of garlic and ginger visible. Transfer the marinade to an airtight container and refrigerate until ready to use.

This marinade will keep, refrigerated, for up to 7 days.

# PICKLED RED ONION

MAKES 1 CUP

## INGREDIENTS

- 1 red onion, very thinly sliced
- 5 cloves garlic, finely sliced
- 1⅓ cups red wine vinegar
- 1 cup granulated sugar
- 1 tablespoon fine sea salt

## DIRECTIONS

Place the sliced onion and garlic in a large heatproof jug or glass container (for example, Pyrex).

Combine the vinegar, sugar, and salt in a saucepan and bring to a simmer over medium heat, stirring regularly to dissolve the sugar and salt.

Pour the hot liquid over the onions and garlic and set aside to cool. Cover and refrigerate until ready to use. The pickled onion will keep, refrigerated, for up to 1 week.

# BAO BUNS

**MAKES 15 BUNS
(SERVE 2 OR MORE
WITH EACH SALAD)**

## YOU WILL NEED:

- Digital scale
- Chopstick
- Parchment paper cut into fifteen 3-inch squares
- Bamboo steamer

## INGREDIENTS

- 2¼ cups (265 g) all-purpose flour, plus more for dusting
- ¼ teaspoon fine sea salt
- 1 teaspoon instant yeast
- 2 tablespoons granulated sugar
- 1½ teaspoons baking powder
- 2 tablespoons whole milk
- ½ cup (125 ml) warm water
- 1 tablespoon avocado oil, plus more for brushing and for the chopstick

## DIRECTIONS

In the bowl of a stand mixer fitted with the dough hook, combine the flour, salt, yeast, sugar, and baking powder. In a large measuring jug, combine the milk, warm water, and avocado oil. With the machine running on low speed, slowly pour the milk and water mixture into the dry ingredients. Let the mixer run for 2 minutes until the ingredients are well combined. Increase the mixing speed to medium and mix for another 2 minutes until the dough has a smooth yet tacky feel to it.

Dust the dough with a tablespoon or two of flour, and use your hands to shape it into a ball, kneading it a few times on the counter. Clean the mixer bowl well, then lightly coat it with a little oil. Return the dough to the bowl and cover with a damp cloth. Set the dough aside to proof in a warm, moist, draft-free location (inside a microwave next to a jug of boiled water works well!).

Once the dough has doubled in size, 1½ to 2 hours, turn it out onto the counter and knead it a few times to release some of the air. Use a scale to portion the dough into 15 balls. Each ball should weigh about 30 grams (or weigh your dough, then divide that number by 15 to determine the desired weight of each ball)—this dough is very forgiving, so if you've estimated incorrectly, you can add or subtract dough as needed, and just give the ball a little kneading to incorporate any additional dough. Cover the balls with plastic wrap or a damp tea towel.

Use a rolling pin to flatten out each ball, one at a time, into an oval shape, about 4 to 5 inches long. Brush the surface lightly with the avocado oil. Oil the chopstick lightly and lay it across the center of each oval then fold the oval over the chopstick to form a half-moon-shaped bun. Pull out the chopstick gently from the side of the bun and transfer the bun to a square of parchment paper on a large sheet tray. Cover with plastic wrap or a damp tea towel while you work to shape the remaining buns.

Once you've shaped all the buns, make sure they are completely covered and set aside to rest for 15 to 20 minutes. In the meantime, bring a large pot of water to a boil and set a large bamboo steamer over top.

Working in batches to avoid overcrowding the steamer, steam the buns on the parchment squares for 10 minutes, covered. They are cooked once the dough has puffed up and the buns look like small pillows. The buns can be used immediately or set aside to cool completely, then placed in plastic freezer bags and frozen for up to 2 months. (Reheat as many frozen buns as you need in a steamer for 2 to 3 minutes, until puffy, soft, and warmed all the way through.)

# Legally Blonde Salad

◦ SERVES 1 ◦

In French market cuisine the mind-set is to pair ingredients locally, seasonally, and logically. What that means is, if you are, say, cooking rabbit, then a logical pairing is to serve it accompanied by mustard greens, lettuce, and maybe even sliced turnips. Serve rabbit with what a rabbit eats. Simple, delicious, makes sense.

And so, with our Legally Blonde salad, we wanted to create a salad full of cannabis cravings, per our experience. That meant old Canadian cheddar, all-dressed chips—our equivalent is pita chips with Cajun seasoning—chia and hemp (of course) seeds, reassuringly good lettuce and creamy avocado. And a CBD oil–based dressing.

It's interesting to note that when we were conceiving this half-baked idea, cannabis had just become legal in Quebec. It took us months to buy the CBD oil at our local SQDC (the government-run cannabis sales outlet) as it was constantly sold out in Quebec and in Ontario. Just to say, if you don't have a stash, plan ahead!

## INGREDIENTS

- ◦ 2 cups mesclun greens
- ◦ 2 cups kale or lamb's lettuce
- ◦ 2 tablespoons chia seeds
- ◦ 2 tablespoons hemp seeds
- ◦ 1 apple, thinly sliced
- ◦ ¼ cup grated old cheddar or Canadian sharp cheddar
- ◦ ½ cup Homemade Pita Chips (page 150) tossed in Cajun Seasoning (page 149)
- ◦ ¼ cup Mock Chicken (page 142) (optional)
- ◦ ½ avocado, diced
- ◦ 1 fried egg, for garnish

- ◦ ⅓ cup CBD Dressing (page 165)

## DIRECTIONS

Combine all of the ingredients except the fried egg in a large stainless-steel bowl. Top with the dressing, and using tongs, toss until well mixed and dressed. Garnish with the fried egg.

# Spicy Smoke Show Salad

◦ SERVES 1 ◦

When Dave Rose, our good friend and producer of the legendary Smoke Show sauce, approached us about using his smoked jalapeño hot sauce at Mandy's, we were so excited to figure out a signature salad that would showcase how delicious it is. Meet the Spicy Smoke Show Salad, a spin-off from our Mexi Salad with added olives, onions, more fresh cilantro, grated sharp cheddar, and diced crunchy bell peppers. This salad feels like eating nachos, but it's healthy! Trust us when we say it might become your new Super Bowl go-to platter!

## INGREDIENTS

- 2 cups chopped romaine lettuce
- 2 cups mesclun greens
- ½ avocado, diced
- ¼ cup diced red and green bell peppers
- ¼ cup canned corn kernels, drained and rinsed
- ¼ cup canned black beans, drained and rinsed
- ¼ cup grated sharp cheddar
- 2 tablespoons pitted Kalamata olives
- 2 tablespoons thinly sliced red onion
- 1 tablespoon torn cilantro leaves and stems
- ½ cup crushed corn tortilla chips

- ⅓ cup Smoke Show Dressing (page 170)

## DIRECTIONS

Combine all of the ingredients in a large stainless-steel bowl. Top with the dressing, and using tongs, toss until well mixed and dressed.

# Miso, Salmon, and Noodle Salad

∘ SERVES 1 ∘

MANDY | When I was a kid, I detested salmon—abhorred it. I can still remember the taste of school cafeteria overcooked dry salmon with no seasoning and its permeating fishy smell. When I learned that salmon could actually be incredibly rich and fatty and delicate and flaky if cooked and served right, I was determined to make a salad with it. For this one, I lean on some East Asian influences: loads of fresh herbs, a mouth-puckering yet sweet addition of pickled broccoli stems (why only use the florets? Thanks for this addition, Lachie!), some gluten-free rice noodles to fill you up a bit more, and a lime chili dressing to send it all over the top.

## INGREDIENTS

- 1 cup mesclun greens
- 1 cup arugula
- ½ cup Rice Noodles (page 201)
- ½ avocado, diced
- ¼ cup shredded carrot
- ¼ cup thinly sliced red cabbage
- ¼ cup Pickled Broccoli Stems (page 107)
- 2 tablespoons black and white sesame seeds
- 2 tablespoons torn basil leaves
- 2 tablespoons torn mint leaves
- 2 tablespoons torn cilantro leaves
- ¼ pound Roasted Marinated Salmon (page 107), skin off

- ⅓ cup Lime Chili Thai Dressing (page 162)

## DIRECTIONS

Combine all of the ingredients except the salmon in a large stainless-steel bowl. Top with the dressing, and using tongs, toss until well mixed and dressed. Transfer to a serving bowl and arrange the salmon, broken into large flaky pieces, over top.

## PICKLED BROCCOLI STEMS

MAKES 1½ CUPS
(6 PORTIONS)

### INGREDIENTS

- 10 ounces broccoli stems (about 4 stems, peeled and trimmed)
- 1 cup granulated sugar
- 1⅓ cups rice wine vinegar
- 2 tablespoons lime juice
- 2 teaspoons sesame oil
- 2 tablespoons minced garlic

### DIRECTIONS

Slice the broccoli stems very thinly using a mandoline, or do like we do at Mandy's and spiralize them!

Place the sliced broccoli stems in a heatproof quart-size Mason jar or two 2-cup jars.

In a small saucepan, combine the sugar, vinegar, lime juice, sesame oil, and garlic and bring to a boil over medium heat. Stir until the sugar is completely dissolved, about 2 minutes. Pour over the broccoli stems, then set aside to cool. Cover and refrigerate for 1 hour.

The pickled stems will keep, refrigerated, for up to 1 week.

## ROASTED MARINATED SALMON

MAKES 1 POUND SALMON
(4 PORTIONS)

### INGREDIENTS

- 1-pound organic salmon fillet (we use Atlantic), center cut, skin on
- 3 tablespoons avocado oil
- 2 tablespoons white miso
- 2 tablespoons tamari
- 2 tablespoons rice wine vinegar
- 2 tablespoons lime juice
- 1 tablespoon lemon juice
- 1 tablespoon minced garlic
- 1 tablespoon minced ginger
- 2 teaspoons Sriracha sauce
- 2 teaspoons sambal oelek

NOTE: THIS RECIPE YIELDS FOUR PORTIONS OF COOKED SALMON; TO INCREASE THE YIELD TO SIX PORTIONS, USE 1½ POUNDS OF SALMON AND THE SAME AMOUNT OF MARINADE, INCREASING THE COOKING TIME BY 7 MINUTES OR SO.

### DIRECTIONS

Place the salmon in a glass container, skin side down.

To prepare the marinade, combine all the ingredients in a small bowl until well blended.

Coat the salmon with the marinade. Refrigerate overnight or for a minimum of 12 hours. We marinate our salmon for 24 hours.

Preheat the oven to 375°F.

Lay the marinated salmon on a parchment-lined sheet tray. Roast for 25 minutes until the flesh looks firm but still juicy, or until the internal temperature of the fish in its thickest part registers 145°F on an instant-read digital thermometer. Cool at room temperature then refrigerate in an airtight container. The roasted salmon will keep for up to 5 days.

# Clean Green Salad

◦ SERVES 1 ◦

Often, Mandy's will have a customer who wants only veggies—for whatever reason: they ate too much, they're on a detox, they're you-name-it–intolerant—and so they come in search of strictly raw greens. And so, if you want it, you get it! This recipe is a clean, green, and mean but healthy salad to tick all those boxes. We love adding avocado to pretty much everything, but if you're watching your calorie intake, feel free to omit it.

## INGREDIENTS

- 2 cups chopped romaine lettuce
- 2 cups mesclun greens
- ¼ cup thinly sliced red cabbage
- ¼ cup small broccoli florets (raw)
- ¼ cup diced cucumber
- ¼ cup (thawed and rinsed) frozen edamame
- ¼ cup sliced scallion (green part only)
- ¼ cup pumpkin seeds
- 2 tablespoons torn basil leaves
- 2 tablespoons torn mint leaves
- 2 tablespoons torn cilantro leaves
- ½ avocado, diced (optional)

- ⅓ cup Spring Detox Dressing (page 169)

## DIRECTIONS

Combine all of the ingredients in a large stainless-steel bowl. Top with the dressing, and using tongs, toss until well mixed and dressed.

# The Kaiser (Vegan Caesar)

◦ SERVES 1 ◦

Caesar may be the emperor of North American salads, but we wanted to accommodate our vegan customers with similar flavors but without the bacon, eggs, mayo, and anchovies. Blessed with the silkiness of a blended tofu dressing and the umami of nutritional yeast, this salad has the same creaminess as a traditional Caesar but with the added Middle Eastern touch of fresh mint and parsley, as well as the addition of a *shish taouk–* inspired marinated "mock" chicken made from nutritional yeast, tamari sauce, and tofu—a creation from Mandy's head chef Lachlan McGillivray. The mock chicken is like vegan KFC popcorn chicken. Highly addictive.

## INGREDIENTS

- 2 cups chopped romaine lettuce
- 2 cups shredded lacinato kale
- ¼ cup canned green lentils, drained and rinsed
- ¼ cup cherry tomatoes, halved
- ¼ cup diced cucumber
- ½ avocado, cubed
- 2 tablespoons pomegranate seeds (optional)
- 2 tablespoons sliced scallion (green part only)
- 2 tablespoons chopped flat-leaf parsley
- 2 teaspoons torn mint leaves
- ½ cup Homemade Pita Chips (page 150)
- ½ cup Mock Chicken (page 142)
- ⅓ cup Kaiser Dressing (page 157)

## DIRECTIONS

Combine all of the ingredients in a large stainless-steel bowl. Top with the dressing, and using tongs, toss until well mixed and dressed.

# Ladies Who Lunch

At Mandy's there are two factors that we take into consideration when selecting wine.

The first is thinking about wine as a food itself. Fresh salads and fresh produce call for honest fresh wines. We choose small organic producers with delicious, easy, fulfilling wines that represent generosity more than showmanship. At lunch, we want something thirst-quenching with a short, snappy finish; something that is energizing enough to allow us to carry on with our day, rather than finishing with a long lingering rich texture that may feel heavy. Something that's easy for the body to integrate is great, so lower alcohol is ideal.

The second is the flavor pairing. Salad dressing is the elixir that brightens up and brings alive all the amazing vegetables and ingredients in your salad, but it can quickly overpower the subtle flavors of wine. For a salad with a dressing containing a certain dose of acidity, we recommend an equally energetic wine. For red wines, to keep it fresh, we opt for colder-climate, lower-tannin, brighter reds, such as the amazing wines of Angélique Quentin Bourse in Azay-le-Rideau.

Here are a few other bottles we serve at our Old Port location. Keep an eye out for these:

- Cucú Cantaba La Ran Verdejo (white)
- Gregoletto Verdiso (white)
- Succés Experiència Parellada (white)
- Succés La Cuca de Llum (red)
- Le Sot de l'Ange Quentin Bourse (red)
- Le Sot de l'Ange Sottise (rosé)

# Cajun Shrimp Salad

∘ SERVES 1 ∘

We first gave this salad a test run at our Old Montreal location in the summer of 2017, and it hasn't left the menu since. The marriage of smoky multilayered Cajun shrimp mixed with hints of lime, cilantro, mango, and salty bacon brings a little of Louisiana all the way up to Montreal.

## INGREDIENTS

- 5 fresh jumbo (16/20) shrimp, peeled and deveined
- 1 teaspoon Cajun Seasoning (page 149)
- 2 tablespoons olive oil
- Juice of ½ lime
- 2 cups baby spinach
- 2 cups mesclun greens
- 2 slices bacon, cut into pieces and fried until crispy
- ½ ripe Ataulfo mango, diced
- ½ avocado, diced
- ½ cup halved cherry tomatoes
- 1 tablespoon torn cilantro leaves
- 1 tablespoon sliced scallion (green part only)

- ⅓ cup Cilantro Lime Ginger Dressing (page 171)

## DIRECTIONS

In a small bowl, toss the shrimp with the Cajun Seasoning. In a frying pan over medium-high heat, heat the olive oil until shimmering.

Fry the shrimp for 2 to 3 minutes, turning them once or twice, then splash with the lime juice and remove from the heat.

Combine the shrimp with the spinach, mesclun, bacon, mango, avocado, cherry tomatoes, cilantro, and scallion in a large stainless-steel bowl. Top with the dressing, and using tongs, toss until well mixed and dressed.

# Peach and Prosciutto Salad

◦ SERVES 1 ◦

Juicy summer peaches. Peppery olive oil. San Daniele prosciutto. A ball of burrata cut into its middle, oozing its creamy, cheesy glory. Are you drooling yet? You get the idea. This salad is best served on a hot summer day with a carafe of ice-cold white wine (see our wine guide on page 111) and looks lovely when served on a platter.

NOTE: IF YOU WANT TO MAKE USE OF A WHOLE BALL OF BURRATA, THIS SALAD WILL SERVE FOUR PEOPLE. JUST BE SURE TO MULTIPLY THE OTHER INGREDIENTS BY FOUR ALSO.

## INGREDIENTS

- 1 cup arugula
- 1 cup shredded frisée lettuce
- 1 cup chopped radicchio
- 1 peach, cut into 6 or 8 segments
- 2 tablespoons thinly sliced red onion
- ¼ ball fresh burrata, at room temperature
- 2 tablespoons toasted pine nuts
- 2 tablespoons torn basil leaves
- 2 thin slices prosciutto

- ⅓ cup Italian Summer Dressing (page 155)

## DIRECTIONS

Combine all of the ingredients except the prosciutto in a large stainless-steel bowl. Top with the dressing, and using tongs, toss until well mixed and dressed. Serve on a large plate or small platter, and top with the prosciutto slices.

# Santorini Salad

◦ SERVES 1 ◦

We adore Greek food, especially the simplicity of its flavors and the inherent health of the Mediterranean diet. We think of blinding white architecture framing azure blue skies, and the best, freshest produce. Okay, we also threw in some rosemary spiced nuts because, well, we adore them too. And we turned blueberries, raspberries, and strawberries into a salad dressing. This whole combination is a mix of super sweet and tart and super salty, with some cayenne kick to those herbed nuts and a berry blitz of a dressing. Trust us, it works.

## INGREDIENTS

- 3 cups mesclun greens
- 1 cup chopped radicchio
- ½ cup Red Quinoa (page 201)
- ½ cup cubed watermelon
- ¼ cup cubed feta
- ¼ cup Spicy Rosemary Nuts (page 147)
- 2 tablespoons thinly sliced red onion
- 2 tablespoons torn mint leaves
- 2 tablespoons torn basil leaves

- ⅓ cup Berry Good Dressing (page 164)

## DIRECTIONS

Combine all of the ingredients except for the mint and basil in a large stainless-steel bowl. Top with the dressing, and using tongs, toss until well mixed and dressed. Serve on a large plate or small platter. Garnish the salad with the basil and mint leaves.

# Spring Farro Salad

◦ SERVES 1 ◦

Inspired by NYC's Charlie Bird restaurant's famed and delicious farro salad, we've taken its scrumptious base of fluffy apple cider–braised farro and tossed it with zingy tart berries, salty hard Parmesan, and of course, a whackload of greens and fresh herbs.

## INGREDIENTS

- 2 cups mesclun greens
- 1 cup shredded curly kale
- 1 cup arugula
- ½ cup Dressed Farro (page 200)
- ¼ cup halved cherry tomatoes
- ¼ cup thinly sliced radishes
- 2 tablespoons blueberries (optional)
- ¼ cup Parmesan flakes
- 2 tablespoons chopped pistachio nuts
- 1 tablespoon toasted pecans
- 2 tablespoons torn mint leaves
- 2 tablespoons torn basil leaves
- Lemon juice, for drizzling
- Walnut or hazelnut oil, for drizzling

## DIRECTIONS

Combine all of the ingredients except the lemon juice and walnut oil in a large stainless-steel bowl. Using tongs, toss until well mixed, then adjust the taste with a splash of lemon juice and a dash of walnut oil as needed.

# Sweet and Salty Fennel Salad

◦ SERVES 1 ◦

MANDY | I don't quite remember where I was when I first tasted the combination of shaved fennel and fresh orange in a salad (but definitely at an Italian restaurant somewhere on the Main—St-Laurent Boulevard, back in the day), but my taste buds were very intrigued. Combine those delicate anise and citrus flavors with some salty olives and crispy bacon . . . Delish!

## INGREDIENTS

- 1 ruby red grapefruit
- 1 navel orange
- 2 cups mesclun greens
- ½ fennel bulb, cored and sliced very thin using a mandoline (about 2 cups sliced)
- 2 slices bacon, cut into pieces and fried until crispy
- 1 tablespoon coarsely chopped Castelvetrano olives
- 1 tablespoon minced fennel fronds
- 1 tablespoon torn mint leaves
- 1 tablespoon torn basil leaves

- ⅓ cup Honey Citrus Dressing (page 163)

## DIRECTIONS

Peel and segment the grapefruit and the orange: using a sharp paring knife, cut away the peel and white pith from the fruit until only the orange or ruby red flesh remains, then working over a small bowl to catch the juice, cut out the individual segments, discarding the fruit's leftover membranes when done. (You can use the juice as part of the Honey Citrus Dressing.)

Combine all of the ingredients including the citrus segments in a large stainless-steel bowl. Top with the dressing, and using tongs, toss until well mixed and dressed.

# Poutine Food Truck Salad

◦ SERVES 1 ◦

MANDY | For years, we had dreamed of joining the hip and hardworking restaurants that had acquired greasy, party-going food trucks. And in the early spring of 2017, we finally got our very own truck. True to style, we wrapped that baby up in bright pink with gold-foil palm trees and rolled into festivals like Osheaga, Jazz Fest, and Montreal's Just for Laughs. We needed something to compete with the sloppy joes, tacos, and other fatty grub being served by our food truck compadres, maybe even an homage to a Quebec classic. And that's how our poutine salad was born. Instead of French fries (which could get soggy quite quickly), we opted for potatoes (with an added garnish of crunchy potato chips atop). Due to portion size of the Gravy Potatoes—and deliciousness—we recommend scaling up the salad ingredients and serving this for two or more.

NOTE: THE CHICKEN GRAVY YIELDS FOUR CUPS. YOU'LL NEED TWO CUPS FOR THE SALAD AND MOST OF THE REST FOR THE MAPLE GRAVY DRESSING (PAGE 163).

## INGREDIENTS

- 4 cups chopped romaine lettuce
- ½ cup Gravy Potatoes (page 124)
- ⅓ cup fresh cheese curds
- 2 tablespoons shredded mozzarella
- 2 slices bacon, cut into pieces and fried until crispy
- ¼ cup kettle-cooked chips (we like Cape Cod)

- ⅓ cup Maple Gravy Dressing (page 163)

## DIRECTIONS

Combine all of the ingredients in a large stainless-steel bowl. Top with the dressing, and using tongs, toss until well mixed and dressed.

## GRAVY POTATOES

MAKES 4 CUPS
(6 TO 8 PORTIONS)

### INGREDIENTS

- 2 pounds small russet potatoes, skin on, each cut into 8 wedges
- ¼ cup olive oil
- 2 teaspoons fine sea salt
- ½ teaspoon freshly ground black pepper
- 2 cups Chicken Gravy (see below)

### DIRECTIONS

Preheat the oven to 450°F.

In a large bowl, toss the potatoes with the oil, salt, and pepper, then spread out evenly on a baking tray.

Bake for 20 minutes until the potatoes start to become golden. Remove from the oven and drizzle the potatoes evenly with the gravy, using a spatula to flip them over and coat them completely.

Bake for a further 10 minutes until gooey and crispy around the edges. Remove from the oven and cool slightly for 3 to 4 minutes before using.

## CHICKEN GRAVY

MAKES ABOUT 4 CUPS

NOTE: AT MANDY'S, WE USE BERTHELET'S PREPREPARED HOT CHICKEN SAUCE MIX.

### INGREDIENTS

- 4 cups water
- 1 cup (100 g) hot chicken sandwich gravy mix

### DIRECTIONS

Bring the water to a boil.

In a large bowl or Pyrex jug, combine 2 cups of the hot water with the gravy powder and whisk until completely dissolved. Add the remaining water and then pour the mixture into a saucepan and, whisking continuously, simmer over medium heat for 5 minutes, until thickened.

# Our Top 10
## Montreal Poutine Spots

La Banquise

La Roulotte

Nouveau Système

Chez Claudette

Restaurant AA

Paul Patates

Green Spot

Patati Patata

Ma Poule Mouillée

Orange Julep

# Keto Salad

## ◦ SERVES 1 ◦

Sometime in 2018, someone you knew, somewhere, was touched by the keto craze. "Are you on keto?" "Is that keto-friendly?" "I fell off the keto wagon . . ." and on and on. The ketogenic diet is basically an extremely low-sugar, low-carbohydrate diet, with a focus on plentiful amounts of dark greens, protein, and healthy fats. We had all the fixings to make a delicious filling salad to satisfy the keto craze, and we featured one as a monthly special. It was a hit, one that we bring back in the spring, when it starts to be "summer bod" game time. Oh, yes.

## INGREDIENTS

- 4 cups mesclun greens
- 1 avocado, diced
- ½ cup diced cucumber
- ¼ cup thinly sliced button mushrooms
- ¼ cup sliced canned hearts of palm
- ¼ cup Roasted Chicken Breast (page 149)
- 2 slices bacon, cut into pieces and fried until crispy
- ¼ cup Parmesan flakes
- 2 tablespoons sliced scallion (green part only)
- 2 tablespoons torn basil leaves
- 2 tablespoons tarragon leaves

- ⅓ cup Keto Caesar Dressing (see note on page 156)

## DIRECTIONS

Combine all of the ingredients in a large stainless-steel bowl. Top with the dressing, and using tongs, toss until well mixed and dressed.

# Filet Mignon Salad

○ SERVES 1 ○

A few years ago, it felt like we had covered most of the expected protein options for salads: chicken, salmon, tuna, bacon, lobster . . . but we hadn't yet tackled steak. When we opened our downtown Crescent Street location in April 2015, we wanted to be sure we welcomed ALL eaters: vegans, vegetarians, omnivores, pescatarians, and yes, carnivores (who love salad too!). And so it was *bienvenue* to the Filet Mignon Salad. Picture a business lunch at a gourmet steak house in Montreal (Gibbys! Moishes! Rib 'N Reef!): juicy beef tenderloin without the heavy mashed potatoes or fries on the side.

## INGREDIENTS

- 2 cups baby spinach
- 1 cup arugula
- 1 cup mesclun greens
- ½ avocado, sliced
- ½ cup halved cherry tomatoes
- 2 tablespoons thinly sliced red onion
- 1 tablespoon torn tarragon leaves
- ¼ pound Seared Filet Mignon, sliced

- ⅓ cup Blue Ranch Dressing (page 171)

## DIRECTIONS

Combine all of the ingredients except for the filet mignon in a large stainless-steel bowl. Top with the dressing, and using tongs, toss until well mixed and dressed. Transfer to a serving bowl and layer the slices of filet mignon on top. Serve while still warm.

# Ceviche Salad

◦ SERVES 1 ◦

In summer 2017, we were asked to participate in a "Summer Chef-Off" at Balnea Spa in the Eastern Townships of Quebec—a nature retreat on a private lake, with hot tubs, massages, saunas, and everything to relax with. About 15 restaurants and chefs had to create a "Spa Salad" one Sunday of the summer, and the guests at Balnea would vote on their favorite. We worked very closely with our head chef, Lachlan McGillivray, who devised a masterful salad of raw fish inspired by Mandy's favorite flavors. We continued to call this the "Spa Salad," as we had a fabulously fun time making this bright salad on a gorgeous summer Sunday with our team out at Balnea, followed by some hot-tubbing and lake jumps. We served this salad exclusively at our Old Montreal location that same summer.

## INGREDIENTS

- 2 cups mesclun greens
- ½ cup Rice Noodles (page 201)
- ¼ pound Marinated Raw Fish (page 132)
- 2 tablespoons diced red bell pepper
- ½ cup Baked Marinated Baby Corn (page 132)
- ½ avocado, diced (optional)
- ¼ cup Pineapple Peanut Pickle (page 133)
- 5 to 6 Plantain Chips (page 133)
- 2 tablespoons torn Thai basil leaves
- 2 tablespoons torn mint leaves
- 2 tablespoons torn cilantro leaves

- ⅓ cup Peanut Sesame Dressing (page 161)

## DIRECTIONS

Place the greens in a bowl. Top with the noodles. Drizzle with the Peanut Sesame Dressing and toss to combine.

Drain the fish. Measure out a ½-cup portion of marinated fish. Toss the fish with the diced pepper and place the mixture in the bowl.

Arrange the baby corn, avocado, pineapple pickle, and plantain chips in the bowl, then top with generous amounts of Thai basil, mint, and cilantro.

# MARINATED RAW FISH

MAKES 4 SALAD PORTIONS

## INGREDIENTS

- 1 pound fresh white ocean fish (for example, grouper, halibut, red snapper, or sea bass), cut into ½-inch cubes
- 6 cloves garlic
- 3 tablespoons coarsely chopped ginger
- ½ cup packed cilantro leaves
- 1½ cups freshly squeezed lime juice (about 15 limes)
- 1 tablespoon fish sauce
- 1 tablespoon sambal oelek
- 1 tablespoon sesame oil
- 1 tablespoon fine sea salt

NOTE: IT IS KEY TO USE THE FRESHEST POSSIBLE FISH AND MARINATE IT THE SAME DAY YOU BUY IT. RAW MARINATED FISH IS ALSO BEST SERVED THE SAME DAY. AS SUCH, IF YOU'RE MAKING A SALAD FOR YOURSELF ONLY, YOU CAN MAKE THE MARINADE AHEAD OF TIME, BUT YOU SHOULD ONLY MARINATE A SMALLER AMOUNT OF FISH (WE RECOMMEND ¼ POUND, OR A BIT LESS, PER PERSON).

THE MARINADE CAN ALSO BE MADE IN A SMALLER BATCH BY DIVIDING AMOUNTS BY THREE: TWO CLOVES GARLIC, 1 TABLESPOON GINGER, ¼ CUP CILANTRO LEAVES, ½ CUP LIME JUICE, AND 1 TEASPOON EACH FISH SAUCE, SAMBAL OELEK, SESAME OIL, AND SALT.

## DIRECTIONS

Place the cubed fish in a glass container or bowl.

In a blender, combine the garlic, ginger, cilantro, lime juice, fish sauce, sambal, sesame oil, and salt. Process on medium-high speed until mostly smooth and well combined, 10 to 15 seconds. Stop the blender and scrape down the sides of the jar with a spatula as needed.

Pour the marinade over the fish, cover, and refrigerate for 2 hours before serving. The marinated fish will keep for up to 24 hours refrigerated.

# BAKED MARINATED BABY CORN

MAKES 4 SALAD PORTIONS

## INGREDIENTS

- ½ cup coconut milk
- ¼ cup tamari
- ¼ cup light brown sugar
- 2 tablespoons fish sauce
- 1 tablespoon lime juice
- One 14-ounce can organic baby corn niblets, drained and rinsed

## DIRECTIONS

Preheat the oven to 375°F.

In a bowl, combine the coconut milk, tamari, sugar, fish sauce, and lime juice. Add the baby corn and mix well. Transfer to a sheet tray and spread out the baby corn pieces.

Bake for 20 minutes, until the sauce thickens and the corn pieces start to become golden. Set aside to cool. Refrigerate in an airtight container until ready to use.

# PINEAPPLE PEANUT PICKLE

MAKES 1 CUP
(4 PORTIONS) PICKLE

## INGREDIENTS

### CHILI SAUCE

- 1 cup granulated sugar
- 1 cup white vinegar
- 10 cloves garlic, minced
- 2 teaspoons togarashi
- 2 teaspoons red bell pepper flakes
- 2 teaspoons fine sea salt

### PINEAPPLE PEANUT PICKLE

- ¼ fresh pineapple, cored and diced
- 1 cup roasted peanuts
- 3 cloves garlic, minced
- 1 tablespoon torn cilantro
- 2 tablespoons Chili Sauce (see above)
- ½ teaspoon fine sea salt

## DIRECTIONS

To make the chili sauce, combine the sugar, vinegar, garlic, togarashi, pepper flakes, and salt in a saucepan. Bring to a boil over medium heat. Simmer and cook for 2 minutes or so, stirring well, until the sugar is fully dissolved.

Remove from the heat and set aside to cool. Refrigerate in an airtight container until ready to use. This will last, refrigerated, for up to 7 days.

To make the pickle, combine the pineapple, peanuts, garlic, cilantro, chili sauce, and salt in a bowl and stir well. Transfer to an airtight container and refrigerate until ready to use. This pickle will keep, refrigerated, for up to 7 days.

# PLANTAIN CHIPS

MAKES 4 SALAD PORTIONS

## YOU WILL NEED:

- Deep-frying thermometer or an instant-read digital thermometer

## INGREDIENTS

- 4 cups avocado oil
- 2 unripe plantains, peeled and sliced thinly (1⁄16 inch) on the bias
- Fine sea salt

## DIRECTIONS

Line a sheet tray with paper towel.

Heat the oil in a large Dutch oven over medium-high heat to 325°F. Gently add half of the plantain slices and cook, stirring regularly with a slotted spoon or a skimmer, until the plantain is pale golden brown, 5 to 7 minutes, adjusting the burner as required to maintain an oil temperature between 300 and 325°F.

Using a slotted spoon or skimmer, transfer the plantain to the sheet tray and sprinkle lightly with salt. Repeat with the remaining batch of plantain slices.

The cooked chips can be stored at room temperature in an airtight container for up to 7 days.

#

• SERVES 1 •

MANDY | Growing up, we had a strong baseball culture in our family and our city—the Montreal Expos are synonymous with childhood summers for many Montrealers. But what the heck does this have to do with souvlaki? Well, my best friend Anika's dad had box seats for every Expos game, and Anika and I would go as often as we could. We would always order a Kojax (Greek fast food) souvlaki with big dollops of tzatziki and fluffy crispy salted French fries to eat. Then we'd scream our heads off at the game.

Montreal is known for its vibrant strong Greek community and food culture, and while there are no more Expos, we still have a ton of Greek restaurants! We wanted to riff off the classic souvlaki I love, and this salad is it.

## INGREDIENTS

- 2 cups shredded iceberg lettuce
- 2 cups chopped romaine lettuce
- ¼ cup halved cherry tomatoes
- ¼ cup diced cucumbers
- ¼ cup pitted Kalamata olives
- ¼ cup cubed feta cheese
- 2 tablespoons dill fronds
- 2 tablespoons diced red onion
- ½ cup Creamy Oregano Chicken (page 147)
- ¼ cup Homemade Garlic and Thyme Pita Chips (page 150)

- ⅓ cup Creamy Greek Dressing (page 169)

## DIRECTIONS

Combine all of the ingredients except the chicken and the pita chips in a large stainless-steel bowl. Top with the dressing, and using tongs, toss until well mixed and dressed. Spoon the chicken and pita chips over top.

# Montreal Travel Tip!

If you're visiting our Belle Province in the fall, our compatriot Martin Picard does a mean apple-themed menu using apples from the orchard near his *cabane à sucre* (sugar shack) in Mirabel. Highlights include cavatelli with apples, sticky apple toffee pudding, apple soufflé, apple sorbet—all of which take our numerous varietals of apple to the next, decadent level. Don't worry, though, slicing apples into a salad is an excellent beginning!

• WOLFE FAMILY CABIN SINCE 1972 •

# September Salad

◦ SERVES 1 ◦

Here in Montreal, we're fortunate to be living on the Apple Belt. Come September, it's full-on apple season all around: apple pressings for ciders, apple pies, and most simply, using apples in salads. We love the crunchy tartness of Quebec apples in combination with the peppery kick of wild arugula.

## INGREDIENTS

- 1 cup sliced leeks
- 1 cup sliced fennel
- 1 cup olive oil
- 1 teaspoon fine sea salt
- 1 teaspoon freshly ground black pepper
- ¼ cup lemon juice
- 2 McIntosh apples, cored, peeled and diced
- 1 cup Quinoa (page 201)
- 1 cup Parmesan shavings
- 1 cup grapes, halved
- ½ cup toasted pine nuts
- ½ cup shaved and sliced celery
- 1 cup wild arugula
- 1 cup mixed greens
- 1 cup chopped romaine lettuce
- 1 cup baby chicory greens

- ⅓ cup Mandy's House Dressing (page 155)

## DIRECTIONS

Preheat the oven to 375°C.

In a bowl, toss the leeks and fennel together with the olive oil, salt, and pepper. Spread out on a sheet tray, then roast until golden brown, about 20 minutes. Remove from the oven and sprinkle with the lemon juice. Let cool to room temperature.

Combine the roasted leeks and fennel with the apples, quinoa, Parmesan, grapes, pine nuts, celery, and the various greens in a large stainless-steel bowl. Top with the dressing, and using tongs, toss until well mixed and dressed.

Us with our
brother, Josh

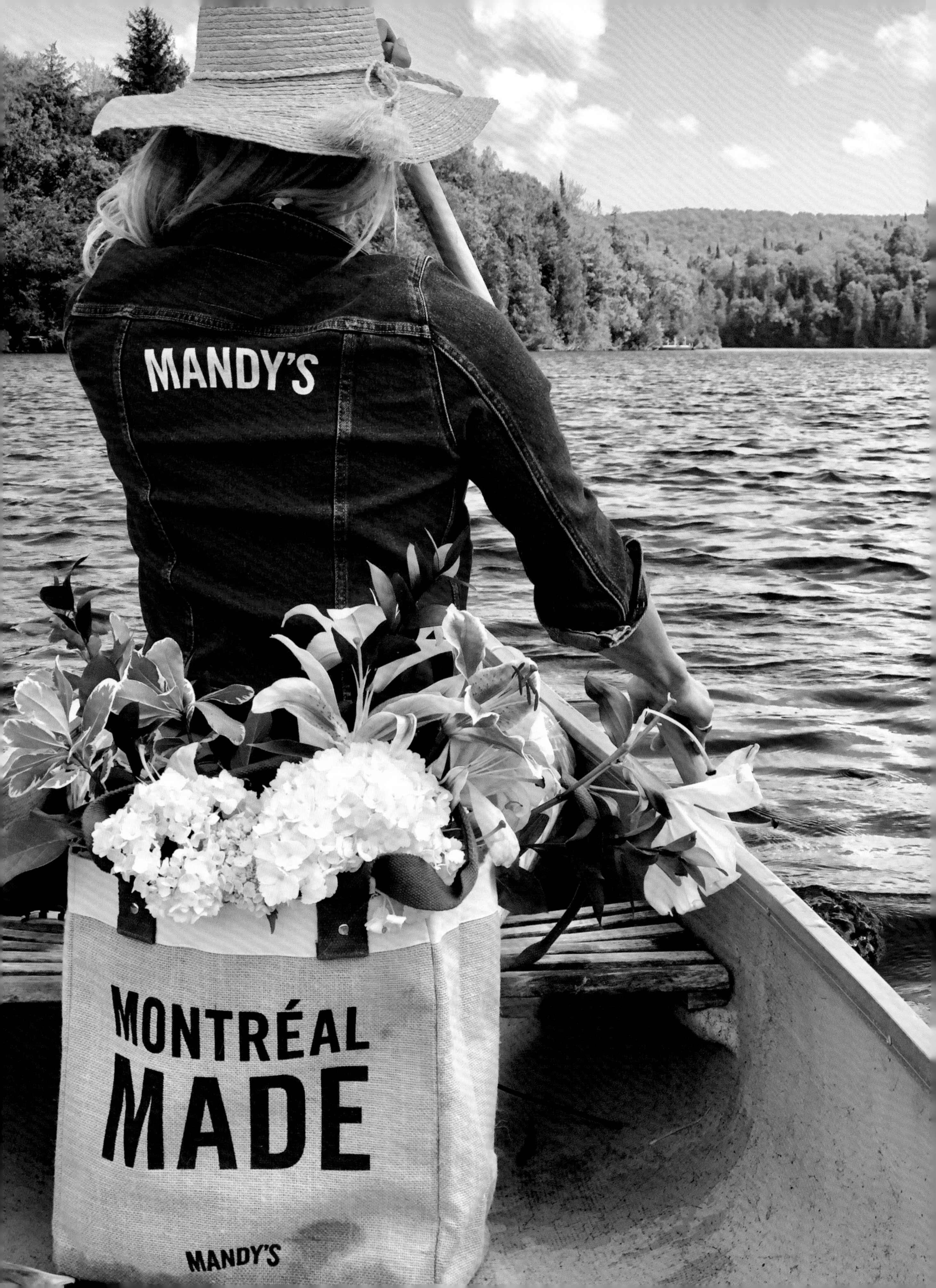
MANDY'S
MONTRÉAL
MADE
MANDY'S

Laurier
location

# SALAD ADDITIONS

The following recipes can be added to almost any of the salads in the book for a bit more substance or crunch.

## MOCK CHICKEN

**MAKES 2 CUPS
(4 PORTIONS)**

### INGREDIENTS

- One 14-ounce (400 g) block firm tofu, unopened
- 2 tablespoons tamari
- 2 tablespoons nutritional yeast flakes
- 1 teaspoon fine sea salt
- ½ teaspoon freshly ground black pepper
- 2 tablespoons avocado oil

MANDY | When I traveled throughout Vietnam in 1999 to 2000, I was astounded by the pervasiveness of Buddhist culture and its influence on Vietnamese cuisine. At that time, I hadn't ever tasted anything like "faux duck" or mock steak, chicken, or shrimp, and it was a revelation! I was a strict vegetarian at the time, and stumbling into tiny nameless roadside shacks that were serving perfectly vegan faux meats was very exciting, both to discover and taste. We've experimented with our own variation for those who crave that texture and the extra veggie-protein boost.

### DIRECTIONS

Place the block of unopened tofu, still in its package, in the freezer for 24 hours or longer.

Defrost the tofu at room temperature until soft and squishy, about 3 hours. This helps the tofu keep its form.

Open the package and drain the tofu over the sink, squeezing and pressing with your hands to remove excess liquid. Then, working over a large bowl, use your hands to crumble the tofu into small bite-size pieces (no longer than 1 inch each).

Toss the crumbled tofu with the tamari, nutritional yeast, salt, and pepper.

In a large frying pan over medium heat, warm the oil. Add the tofu and cook until golden brown, stirring regularly, about 5 minutes.

Remove from the heat, and cool. The mock chicken will keep, refrigerated, in an airtight container for up to 1 week.

# ROASTED MARINATED TEMPEH

MAKES 2 CUPS
(4 PORTIONS)

## INGREDIENTS

- One 8-ounce (240 g) block tempeh
- 3 tablespoons smooth peanut butter
- 3 tablespoons maple syrup
- 2 tablespoons rice wine vinegar
- 2 tablespoons tamari
- 1 tablespoon sesame oil
- Pinch red pepper flakes

When you're a vegetarian, or even if you're just looking for meatless meal options, tofu can start to feel old fast. In comes tempeh, the fermented, meatier (are we allowed to say that?) version of the almighty soy bean. Give this marinated version a try; we promise you will absolutely love it. The key lies in boiling the tempeh before marinating and roasting it, otherwise the marinade won't permeate the protein, and the tempeh will retain a slightly funky (that is, fermented) taste.

NOTE: PEANUT BUTTER ALLERGIES ARE RAMPANT, SO MAKE SURE TO DOUBLE CHECK BEFORE ADDING OUR PB TEMPEH TO ANY SALAD.

## DIRECTIONS

Bring a pot of water to a boil. Lower the heat and simmer the tempeh for 20 minutes until soft. Drain and set the tempeh aside to cool, then cut it into ½-inch cubes.

In a bowl, whisk the peanut butter, maple syrup, vinegar, tamari, sesame oil, and red pepper flakes together until well combined. Stir in the tempeh cubes. Transfer to a ziplock bag and refrigerate for 24 hours.

Preheat the oven to 425°F.

Spread the tempeh cubes out on a sheet tray, discarding any excess marinade. Roast for 5 minutes. Use a spatula to turn the cubes over. Return to the oven and roast for another 5 to 7 minutes until crispy and golden brown.

Set aside to cool at room temperature, then transfer to an airtight container and refrigerate until ready to use.

# ROASTED MEDITERRANEAN SALMON

MAKES 1 POUND OF SALMON
(4 PORTIONS)

## INGREDIENTS

- ⅓ cup coarsely chopped sun-dried tomatoes
- ½ cup dill fronds
- 2 tablespoons diced red onion
- 1 tablespoon brined capers
- 1 teaspoon Dijon mustard
- Zest and juice of 1 lemon
- 1 tablespoon balsamic vinegar
- 1 teaspoon fine sea salt
- 3 tablespoons olive oil
- 1-pound organic salmon fillet (we use Atlantic), center cut, skin on

**NOTE: THIS RECIPE YIELDS FOUR PORTIONS OF COOKED SALMON; TO INCREASE THE YIELD TO SIX PORTIONS, USE 1½ POUNDS SALMON AND THE SAME AMOUNT OF MARINADE, INCREASING THE COOKING TIME BY 7 MINUTES OR SO.**

## DIRECTIONS

To make the salmon marinade, combine all the ingredients except the salmon in a blender and pulse until a thick but fairly smooth paste forms.

Coat the salmon with the marinade and refrigerate for 2 hours or more.

Preheat the oven to 375°F.

Lay the marinated salmon on a parchment-lined sheet tray. Roast for 25 minutes, until the flesh looks firm but still juicy or until the internal temperature of the fish in its thickest part registers 145°F on an instant-read digital thermometer. Cool at room temperature and then refrigerate in an airtight container. The roasted salmon will keep in the fridge for up to 5 days.

# SEARED FILET MIGNON

SERVES 4

## INGREDIENTS

- 1¼ pounds beef tenderloin, cut into three 1-inch-thick steaks
- Fine sea salt and freshly ground pepper
- 2 tablespoons unsalted butter
- 2 tablespoons olive oil

## DIRECTIONS

Season the meat generously with salt and pepper.

Warm the butter and oil in a large frying pan until bubbling and shimmering. Sear the steaks over medium-high heat, cooking for 2 minutes then flipping the steaks over and continuing to cook for approximately 3 more minutes for rare (or until an instant-read digital thermometer registers 120°F), 6 minutes for medium-rare (130°F), or 7 minutes for medium (140°F) doneness.

Set the meat aside to rest for 5 minutes before slicing and layering a quarter of the slices on top of each Filet Mignon salad. If making 1 salad, the remainder of the meat can be stored in an airtight container and refrigerated for up to 5 days.

## ROASTED SWEET POTATO

MAKES 1½ CUPS SWEET POTATO CUBES (6 PORTIONS)

### INGREDIENTS

- 1 large (1-pound) sweet potato
- 1 tablespoon olive oil

### DIRECTIONS

Preheat the oven to 375°F. Slice the sweet potato in half lengthwise. Brush the cut sides with olive oil, then place face down on a small baking sheet.

Bake for 35 to 40 minutes or until the flesh feels tender but not mushy when you insert a small sharp knife into the potato.

Remove from the oven and set aside to cool. Peel off the skin and discard. Cut the sweet potato into ½-inch cubes. The cubes will keep, refrigerated, in an airtight container for up to 5 days.

## PICO DE GALLO

MAKES 2½ CUPS (5 PORTIONS)

### INGREDIENTS

- 4 large Roma tomatoes, halved, cored, seeded, and diced
- ½ cup diced red onion
- ⅓ cup diced jalapeños
- ⅓ cup torn cilantro
- 3 tablespoons lime juice
- 1 teaspoon fine sea salt

### DIRECTIONS

Combine the tomatoes, onion, jalapeño, cilantro, lime juice, and salt in a bowl. Stir to combine. Adjust the salt and lime juice to taste.

Refrigerate in an airtight container until ready to use. This will keep for up to 5 days.

## SHREDDED THAI CHICKEN

MAKES 4 CUPS (6 PORTIONS)

### INGREDIENTS

- 2 tablespoons light brown sugar
- 1 tablespoon minced ginger
- 1 tablespoon tamari
- 1 teaspoon fish sauce
- ¼ teaspoon freshly ground black pepper
- 1 tablespoon grapeseed oil
- 1 teaspoon sesame oil
- 1½ pounds chicken breast

### DIRECTIONS

In a large bowl, use a whisk to combine the brown sugar, ginger, tamari, fish sauce, pepper, grapeseed oil, and sesame oil.

Transfer the chicken breast to a ziplock bag and pour the marinade into the bag. Seal, removing all of the air, and refrigerate for at least 2 hours.

Preheat the oven to 375°F.

Place the chicken breasts on a parchment-lined sheet tray and roast until an instant-digital thermometer registers an internal temperature of 165°F or more, about 30 minutes.

Transfer to a rack to cool. Using two forks, shred the meat into bite-size pieces. The cooked meat will keep, refrigerated, in an airtight container for up to 5 days.

# SPICY ROSEMARY NUTS

**MAKES 4 CUPS
(16 PORTIONS)**

## INGREDIENTS

- ¾ cup pecans
- ¾ cup walnuts
- 1 cup cashews
- 1 cup almonds
- 2 tablespoons olive oil
- 2 sprigs rosemary, leaves chopped fine
- ½ teaspoon Cajun Seasoning (page 149)
- ½ teaspoon red pepper flakes
- 2 teaspoons light brown sugar
- 1 teaspoon fine sea salt

## DIRECTIONS

Preheat the oven to 350°F.

In a large bowl, combine the pecans, walnuts, cashews, and almonds with the olive oil, rosemary, Cajun seasoning, red pepper flakes, sugar, and salt. Mix well until the nuts are evenly coated.

Spread the nuts on a large sheet tray. Bake for 12 minutes, removing the tray from the oven at the halfway point to turn the nuts, until golden brown. Allow to cool to room temperature. Place in an airtight container and store in a cool place. These will keep for up to 2 months.

# CREAMY OREGANO CHICKEN

**MAKES 1½ TO 2 CUPS
(3 TO 4 PORTIONS)**

## INGREDIENTS

- 1½ cups Roasted Chicken Breast (page 149)
- ¼ cup plain Greek yogurt
- ¼ cup mayonnaise
- 2 teaspoons minced oregano leaves
- 1 teaspoon minced garlic
- Fine sea salt and freshly ground black pepper

## DIRECTIONS

Combine the chicken breast in a large bowl with the yogurt, mayonnaise, oregano, and garlic, tossing well to coat evenly. Adjust the seasoning to taste with salt and pepper.

# ROASTED MARINATED TOFU

**MAKES 2 CUPS TOFU CUBES (4 PORTIONS)**

## INGREDIENTS

- 3 tablespoons avocado oil
- 2 tablespoons white miso
- 2 tablespoons tamari
- 2 tablespoons rice wine vinegar
- 2 tablespoons lime juice
- 2 tablespoons maple syrup
- 1 tablespoon lemon juice
- 1 tablespoon minced garlic
- 1 tablespoon minced ginger
- 2 teaspoons Sriracha sauce
- 2 teaspoons sambal oelek
- One 14-ounce (400 g) block firm tofu, cut into ½-inch cubes

Tofu's taste neutrality often works against it—on its own it is not exactly the gold medal winner in the flavor category. But the flip side to that is it's a terrific sponge for absorbing other flavors. We douse ours in a trifecta of sweet, salty, and citrus for the best of all worlds.

**NOTE: THE TOFU SHOULD BE MARINATED OVERNIGHT OR LONGER. PLAN ACCORDINGLY.**

## DIRECTIONS

In a bowl, combine the oil, miso, tamari, vinegar, lime juice, maple syrup, lemon juice, garlic, ginger, Sriracha, and sambal oelek. Whisk until well blended.

Place the tofu cubes in a large ziplock bag and pour the marinade into the bag. Seal well, removing any air from the bag and making sure all the cubes are coated. Refrigerate overnight or up to 24 hours.

Preheat the oven to 425°F.

Lay the cubes on a large sheet tray (not lined with parchment paper), spreading them out, and roast for 5 minutes. Discard any leftover marinade. Remove the tray from the oven, turn over the cubes of tofu, and roast for another 5 minutes. Turn the cubes one more time, and roast for a final 3 minutes or until all the tofu is golden brown and crispy. Set the tray aside. When the tofu has cooled completely, refrigerate in an airtight container until ready to use. The cubed tofu will keep for up to 5 days.

# JAMMY EGG

**MAKES 1 EGG**

## INGREDIENTS

- 1 egg

## DIRECTIONS

Place an egg in a small saucepan and cover with cold water. Bring to a rolling boil. Remove from the heat, cover the pot, and let stand for 8 to 10 minutes. Pour out all the hot water and rinse with cold water until the egg cools to room temperature, about 2 minutes. We call this "jammy" because the yolk is not 100 percent set, resulting in a smooth and creamy texture.

# ROASTED CHICKEN BREAST

## MAKES 1½ CUPS CUBED CHICKEN (6 PORTIONS)

### INGREDIENTS

- 1 large (10 ounces) skinless boneless chicken breast
- 1 tablespoon olive oil
- 1 teaspoon Montreal steak spice or your preferred steak spice

When we first started out, we roasted our chicken off-site (that is, in our apartments). We were always experimenting with different flavor combinations but soon realized we just needed one standard neutral flavor that was juicy and tasty. So we created a super simple dry rub of kosher salt, cracked peppercorns, dehydrated garlic, and bell peppers. But then we realized this was just . . . steak spice! So now we use steak spice from local legends Joe Beef (available everywhere in Canada). This chicken is very useful to have on hand in the fridge for adding to any salad during the week.

**NOTE: THIS MAKES ENOUGH FOR 6 SALADS. FOR THE STEAK SPICE, WE LIKE TO USE THE JOE BEEF BUTCHER'S BLEND.**

### DIRECTIONS

Preheat the oven to 390°F.

Rub the chicken breast with the oil and the steak spice. Place on a small parchment-lined sheet tray and roast until the internal temperature registers 165°F on an instant-read digital thermometer, about 25 minutes.

Set aside to cool. Then cut into ½-inch cubes. The cubed chicken will keep, refrigerated, in an airtight container for up to 5 days.

# CAJUN SEASONING

## MAKES ½ CUP

### INGREDIENTS

- 2 tablespoons + 2 teaspoons salt
- 1 tablespoon cayenne pepper
- 1 tablespoon garlic powder
- 1 tablespoon paprika
- 1 teaspoon onion powder
- 1 teaspoon dried oregano
- 1 teaspoon dried thyme
- 1 teaspoon freshly ground black pepper

This seasoning can be used to spice up Mock Chicken (page 142), Roasted Marinated Tofu (page 148), and has delicious applications in Spicy Rosemary Nuts (page 147), the Cajun Shrimp Salad (page 113) and our Homemade Pita Chips (page 150).

### DIRECTIONS

Combine all of the ingredients in a small bowl and then transfer to an airtight container until ready to use. This spice blend will keep in a cool dark place for up to 3 months.

# HOMEMADE PITA CHIPS

MAKES 4 CUPS
(8 PORTIONS)

## INGREDIENTS

∘ 2 thin 6-inch pitas
∘ 3 tablespoons olive oil
∘ Fine sea salt and freshly ground black pepper

These are our go-to crunch snack. At Mandy's you'll find them in at least the following salads: the Cobb (page 87), the Fave (page 53), La Belle (page 46), the R&D Extraordinaire (page 50), the Lumberjack (page 57) . . . but you can add them to any salad that contains avocados or a dressing with enough oomph to be soaked up by the chips. And by no means do you even need a salad to make these—obviously.

## DIRECTIONS

Preheat the oven to 375°F. Line a sheet tray with parchment paper.

On a chopping board, cut the pitas into 8 wedges, then pull each wedge apart to form 2 triangles.

Brush each side of the triangles with olive oil, then arrange on the tray. It's okay if the triangles are very close together. Sprinkle generously with salt and pepper.

Bake for 5 to 6 minutes, then remove the tray from the oven and turn the chips over, and continue to bake until crisp and golden, another 5 minutes. Set aside to cool completely. These chips will keep in an airtight container for up to 1 week.

## VARIATION: HOMEMADE GARLIC AND THYME PITA CHIPS

Follow the recipe as above, but sprinkle the wedges with 1 tablespoon garlic powder and 1 tablespoon dried thyme, as well as the salt and pepper.

# CRISPY RAMEN NOODLES

MAKES 1¼ CUPS
(ABOUT 4 PORTIONS)

## INGREDIENTS

∘ One 3½ ounce (100 g) package instant ramen noodles
∘ 1 tablespoon avocado oil

## DIRECTIONS

Place the block of dry instant ramen noodles in a ziplock bag and crush the noodles into small pieces using a rolling pin or the bottom of a saucepan.

Over medium heat, in a large frying pan, sauté the noodle bits in the avocado oil until crispy and golden, about 3 minutes. Transfer to a paper towel–lined plate to cool.

This crispy topping will keep indefinitely at room temperature in an airtight container.

# CRISPY FRIED SHALLOTS

MAKES 1½ CUPS
(12 PORTIONS)

## INGREDIENTS

- ½ pound (about 6) large shallots
- 4 cups avocado oil

We use these in any recipe that could use a hit of sweetness and crunch. A constant in the Mandy's mise-en-place!

## DIRECTIONS

Peel and slice the shallots into very thin rings using a mandoline or a sharp knife.

Combine the shallots with the oil in a tall, heavy-bottomed saucepan or small Dutch oven.

Heat the oil over medium-high heat. After 3 to 4 minutes, the oil will start to bubble, as the shallots release their water. Lower the heat to medium and continue to cook, stirring from time to time, until the shallots look golden brown and the bubbling subsides, about 8 more minutes.

Transfer to a paper towel–lined plate to drain. The shallots will crisp up as they cool. Transfer to an airtight storage container. These will keep for up to 1 week at room temperature.

# MANDY'S GUACAMOLE

SERVES 4 TO 6
AS A DIP

## INGREDIENTS

- 4 avocados, mashed
- ½ cup torn cilantro leaves
- ½ cup diced red bell pepper
- 2 tablespoons lime juice
- 1 teaspoon onion powder
- 1 teaspoon fine sea salt
- ½ teaspoon freshly ground black pepper
- ¼ teaspoon cayenne
- 1 tablespoon cilantro leaves, for garnish

Here's a recipe that we make from an ingredient that doesn't make it into our salads. Each of our restaurants receives hundreds of fresh avocados EVERY SINGLE DAY. And often riding that avocado ripeness wave is NOT easy, as we are sure you readers at home know even when dealing with your weekly grocery list. You know the rule: a good avocado for guacamole does not a good one for salad make. And so for our overripe avocados, the perfect waste management solution was to turn them into GUAC! We serve it up with organic blue tortilla chips, or our Homemade Pita Chips (page 150), Roasted Chicken Breast (page 149), and Mock Chicken (page 142).

## DIRECTIONS

Combine all of the ingredients except the 1 tablespoon of cilantro in a bowl and stir well. Adjust seasoning to taste and garnish with the remaining cilantro leaves.

*Tamari Dressing
(page 155)*

# Dressings

° CHAPTER THREE °

# A Note from Meredith

Collaborating on the Mandy's cookbook has completely changed my dressings game. I began buying squeeze bottles. I bought blue masking tape and a marker. I started labeling my dressings with the day I made them. And the dressings in my fridge made me want to make more salads. And grain bowls. And Italian deli-meat sandwiches. Just as a vehicle for my dressings. They became an inspiration and an excuse. Akin to setting up a tight mise en place in the restaurant, once you have a couple of pinch-hitter dressings at the ready, prepping the rest of the salad becomes a kind of automatic calling (not too automatic though: always be mindful when using a knife!). In the salad world, nailing dressings is life-changing and habit-forming. The good kind of habit forming.

# MANDY'S HOUSE

MAKES 2 CUPS (500 ML)

## INGREDIENTS

- 2 cloves garlic
- 6 tablespoons (90 ml) apple cider vinegar
- ¼ cup (60 ml) maple syrup
- 1 tablespoon Dijon mustard
- 1¼ cup (300 ml) olive oil
- ½ teaspoon salt
- 1½ teaspoons freshly ground black pepper

## DIRECTIONS

In a blender, combine the garlic, vinegar, maple syrup, and mustard. Process on medium-high speed until smooth and well combined, 15 to 20 seconds. Stop the blender and scrape down the sides of the jar with a spatula as needed.

With the blender running on low speed, slowly drizzle in the olive oil until the dressing is emulsified and thickened, about 30 seconds. Add the salt and pepper, adjusting the seasoning to taste. Transfer the dressing to an airtight container and refrigerate until ready to use.

This dressing will keep, refrigerated, for up to 7 days.

# ITALIAN SUMMER

MAKES 2 CUPS (500 ML)

## INGREDIENTS

- 1½ cups (375 ml) olive oil
- ½ cup (125 ml) high-quality balsamic vinegar
- 1 tablespoon Maldon salt
- 1 teaspoon freshly ground black pepper

## DIRECTIONS

Combine all the ingredients in a jar and then seal and shake to combine.

This dressing will keep in an airtight container, at room temperature, for up to 7 days.

# TAMARI

MAKES 2 CUPS (500 ML)

## INGREDIENTS

- Just under ⅔ cup (155 ml) apple cider vinegar
- 2 tablespoons tamari
- 1 clove garlic
- ½ cup packed (25 g) nutritional yeast flakes
- 1 cup + 3 tablespoons (290 ml) olive oil
- Fine sea salt and freshly ground black pepper

NOTE: PRODUCT-WISE, WE PREFER THE SAN-J GLUTEN FREE TAMARI AND BOB'S RED MILL NUTRITIONAL YEAST FLAKES.

## DIRECTIONS

In a blender, combine the vinegar, tamari, garlic, and nutritional yeast. Process on medium-high speed until smooth and well combined, 20 to 30 seconds. Stop the blender and scrape down the sides of the jar with a spatula as needed.

With the blender running on low speed, slowly drizzle in the olive oil until the dressing is emulsified and thickened, about 30 seconds. Season to taste with the salt and pepper. Transfer the dressing to an airtight container and refrigerate until ready to use.

This dressing will keep, refrigerated, for up to 7 days.

# CAESAR

MAKES 2 CUPS (500 ML)

## INGREDIENTS

- ¼ cup (60 ml) red wine vinegar
- 2 tablespoons lemon juice
- 6 tablespoons (90 ml) store-bought mayonnaise
- ½ cup packed (50 g) grated Parmesan cheese
- 2 teaspoons Dijon mustard
- 1 clove garlic
- ⅞ cup (200 ml) olive oil
- ½ teaspoon fine sea salt
- 1½ teaspoons freshly ground black pepper

NOTE: FOR A KETO VARIATION ON THIS CAESAR DRESSING, REPLACE THE MAYONNAISE WITH 1 EGG AND 1 EGG YOLK AND INCREASE THE OLIVE OIL TO 1 CUP (250 ML). YOU MAY ALSO PREFER TO USE AVOCADO OIL INSTEAD OF OLIVE OIL.

## DIRECTIONS

In a blender, combine the vinegar, lemon juice, mayonnaise, Parmesan, mustard, and garlic.

Process on medium-high speed until smooth and well combined, 15 to 20 seconds. Stop the blender and scrape down the sides of the jar with a spatula as needed.

With the blender running on low speed, slowly drizzle in the olive oil until the dressing is emulsified and thickened, about 30 seconds. Add the salt and pepper, adjusting the seasoning to taste. Transfer the dressing to an airtight container and refrigerate until ready to use.

This dressing will keep, refrigerated, for up to 7 days.

# SWEET SESAME

MAKES 2 CUPS (500 ML)

## INGREDIENTS

- Scant 1 cup (220 ml) sunflower oil
- 2 tablespoons toasted sesame oil
- 1 cup (250 ml) Sweet Sesame Syrup (see below)

NOTE: OUR REGULARS MAY KNOW THIS DRESSING AS ASIAN, BUT IT IS NOW CALLED SWEET SESAME.

## DIRECTIONS

Pour the sunflower oil, sesame oil, and Sweet Sesame Syrup into a large bowl and whisk well to homogenize. Transfer to an airtight container and refrigerate.

This dressing will keep, refrigerated, for at least 7 days.

# SWEET SESAME SYRUP

MAKES 1¼ CUPS (300 ML)

## INGREDIENTS

- ¾ cup (180 ml) agave syrup
- ½ cup (125 ml) apple cider vinegar
- 3 tablespoons tamari

## DIRECTIONS

In a small saucepan, combine the agave and vinegar. Over medium heat, whisking well, bring to a simmer. Remove from the heat and continue to whisk until the liquids are well blended.

Stir in the tamari. The syrup is ready to be used in Sweet Sesame Dressing (see above) or Ginger Wasabi Dressing (page 169).

## KAISER (VEGAN CAESAR)

MAKES 2 CUPS (500 ML)

### INGREDIENTS

○ 1 cup (250 g) silken tofu
○ ⅓ cup (80 ml) lime juice
○ ⅓ cup (16 g) nutritional yeast flakes
○ 5 to 6 cloves garlic
○ 2 teaspoons whole-grain mustard
○ 2 teaspoons capers
○ 2 teaspoons granulated sugar
○ ⅞ cup (200 ml) olive oil
○ 1 teaspoon fine sea salt
○ ¼ teaspoon freshly ground black pepper

### DIRECTIONS

In a blender, combine the tofu, lime juice, nutritional yeast, garlic, mustard, capers, sugar, and olive oil. Process on medium-high speed until smooth and well combined, 20 to 30 seconds. Add the salt and pepper, adjusting the seasoning to taste. Transfer the dressing to an airtight container and refrigerate until ready to use.

This dressing will keep, refrigerated, for up to 7 days.

## TURMERIC TAHINI

MAKES 2 CUPS (500 ML)

### INGREDIENTS

○ ⅓ cup (80 ml) tahini
○ ½ cup (125 ml) water
○ ¼ cup (60 ml) apple cider vinegar
○ Juice of 1 lemon, plus more as needed
○ 1 tablespoon ground turmeric
○ 2 cloves garlic
○ ½ teaspoon toasted sesame oil
○ ⅓ cup packed (8 g) flat-leaf parsley leaves
○ ⅞ cup (200 ml) olive oil
○ ½ teaspoon salt
○ ¼ teaspoon freshly ground black pepper

### DIRECTIONS

In a blender, combine the tahini, water, vinegar, lemon juice, turmeric, garlic, sesame oil, and parsley. Process on medium-high speed until smooth and well combined, 20 to 30 seconds. Stop the blender and scrape down the sides of the jar with a spatula as needed.

With the blender running on low speed, slowly drizzle in the olive oil until the dressing is emulsified and thickened, about 30 seconds. Adjust the consistency of the dressing with a splash of water as needed. Add the salt and pepper, adjusting the seasoning to taste, and add extra lemon juice if needed. Transfer the dressing to an airtight container and refrigerate until ready to use.

This dressing will keep, refrigerated, for up to 7 days.

# GREEN GODDESS

MAKES 1 CUP (250 ML)

## INGREDIENTS

- 2 tablespoons coarsely chopped scallion (white part only)
- ¼ cup packed (15 g) basil leaves
- ½ cup packed (10 g) flat-leaf parsley leaves
- ¼ cup loosely packed (2 g) tarragon leaves
- ¼ cup (60 ml) apple cider vinegar
- 1 teaspoon Dijon mustard
- ½ cup (125 ml) olive oil
- ½ teaspoon fine sea salt
- ¼ teaspoon freshly ground black pepper

## DIRECTIONS

In a blender, combine the chopped scallion, basil, parsley, tarragon, vinegar, and mustard.

Process on medium-high speed until the herbs looked finely chopped and the ingredients are well combined, 15 to 20 seconds. Stop the blender and scrape down the sides of the jar with a spatula as needed.

With the blender running on low speed, slowly drizzle in the olive oil until the dressing is emulsified and thickened, about 30 seconds. Add the salt and pepper, adjusting the seasoning to taste. Transfer the dressing to an airtight container and refrigerate until ready to use.

This dressing will keep, refrigerated, for up to 3 days.

# WILD GODDESS

MAKES 1 CUP (250 ML)

## INGREDIENTS

- ½ cup (125 ml) Green Goddess Dressing (see above)
- ½ cup (125 ml) Wild Sage Dressing (page 161)

NOTE: IF YOU'VE MADE THE DRESSINGS BELOW AHEAD OF TIME, YOU MAY NEED TO SHAKE THEM IN THEIR JAR OR GIVE THEM A QUICK SPIN IN A BLENDER TO RE-EMULSIFY THEM BEFORE MEASURING THEM OUT FOR THIS RECIPE.

## DIRECTIONS

In a blender, combine the 2 dressings and process until well combined, about 10 seconds. Transfer the dressing to an airtight container and refrigerate until ready to use.

This dressing will keep, refrigerated, for up to 3 days.

# GREEN POWER

MAKES 1 CUP (250 ML)

## INGREDIENTS

- ½ cup (125 ml) Green Goddess Dressing (see above)
- ½ cup (125 ml) Tamari Dressing (page 155)

NOTE: IF YOU'VE MADE THE DRESSINGS BELOW AHEAD OF TIME, YOU MAY NEED TO SHAKE THEM IN THEIR JAR OR GIVE THEM A QUICK SPIN IN A BLENDER TO RE-EMULSIFY THEM BEFORE MEASURING THEM OUT FOR THIS RECIPE.

## DIRECTIONS

Combine the 2 dressings in a blender and process until well combined, about 10 seconds. Transfer the dressing to an airtight container and refrigerate until ready to use.

This dressing will keep, refrigerated, for up to 3 days.

## MISO GINGER

**MAKES 2 CUPS (500 ML)**

### INGREDIENTS

- 1 heaping tablespoon (25 g) white miso paste
- ¼ cup (25 g) coarsely chopped ginger
- 7 tablespoons (105 ml) rice vinegar
- Juice of 1 lime
- 1 tablespoon agave syrup
- 1 teaspoon red pepper flakes
- ¼ cup (60 ml) soy sauce
- 2 teaspoons toasted sesame oil
- ⅞ cup (200 ml) sunflower oil

### DIRECTIONS

In a blender, combine the miso, ginger, vinegar, lime juice, agave, red pepper flakes, soy sauce, and sesame oil. Process on medium-high speed until smooth and well combined, 15 to 20 seconds. Stop the blender and scrape down the sides of the jar with a spatula as needed.

With the blender running on low speed, slowly drizzle in the sunflower oil until the dressing is emulsified and thickened, about 30 seconds. Transfer the dressing to an airtight container and refrigerate until ready to use.

This dressing will keep, refrigerated, for up to 7 days.

## SWEET MISO GINGER

**MAKES 2 CUPS (500 ML)**

### INGREDIENTS

- 1 cup (250 ml) Sweet Sesame Dressing (page 156)
- 1 cup (250 ml) Miso Ginger Dressing (see above)

### DIRECTIONS

Combine the 2 dressings in a blender and process until well combined, about 10 seconds. Transfer the dressing to an airtight container and refrigerate until ready to use.

This dressing will keep, refrigerated, for up to 7 days.

## PROVENÇALE VINAIGRETTE

**MAKES 1 CUP (250 ML)**

### INGREDIENTS

- 8 anchovy fillets
- 2 tablespoons Dijon mustard
- 1 teaspoon granulated sugar
- 2 lemons
- 1 shallot, minced
- ½ cup (125 ml) olive oil
- Fine sea salt and freshly ground black pepper

### DIRECTIONS

In a large bowl, use a fork to mash the anchovies, mustard, and sugar to form a coarse paste.

Use a sharp paring knife to remove the peel and white pith from the lemons. Working over the bowl containing the anchovy-mustard paste, cut between the membranes of the lemon to release its segments. Squeeze the remaining juice from the membranes into the bowl and discard the membranes.

Whisk in the shallot, then slowly whisk in the olive oil—the lemon segments will break up naturally as you whisk. Season with salt and pepper to taste.

This dressing will keep, refrigerated, for up to 7 days.

# CHAMPAGNE VINAIGRETTE

MAKES 2 CUPS (500 ML)

## INGREDIENTS

- ½ cup (125 ml) Champagne vinegar
- 3 tablespoons Dijon mustard
- 3 tablespoons granulated sugar
- 1½ cups olive oil
- 1 teaspoon fine sea salt
- ½ teaspoon freshly ground black pepper

## DIRECTIONS

In a blender, combine the vinegar, mustard, and sugar. Process on medium-high speed until smooth and well combined, 15 to 20 seconds. Stop the blender and scrape down the sides of the jar with a spatula as needed.

With the blender running on low speed, slowly drizzle in the olive oil until the dressing is emulsified and thickened, about 30 seconds. Add the salt and pepper, adjusting the seasoning to taste. Transfer the dressing to an airtight container and refrigerate until ready to use.

This dressing will keep, refrigerated, for up to 7 days.

# WILD SAGE

MAKES 1 CUP (250 ML)

## INGREDIENTS

- ¼ cup (60 ml) balsamic vinegar
- 1 tablespoon honey
- 1 tablespoon Dijon mustard
- 2 cloves garlic
- ¼ cup (5 g) sage leaves
- ½ cup (10 g) basil leaves
- Scant ⅔ cup (150 ml) olive oil
- ¼ teaspoon fine sea salt
- ½ teaspoon freshly ground black pepper

## DIRECTIONS

In a blender, combine the vinegar, honey, mustard, garlic, sage, and basil. Process on medium-high speed until smooth and well combined, 20 to 30 seconds. Stop the blender and scrape down the sides of the jar with a spatula as needed.

With the blender running on low speed, slowly drizzle in the olive oil until the dressing is emulsified and thickened, about 30 seconds. Add the salt and pepper, adjusting the seasoning to taste. Transfer the dressing to an airtight container and refrigerate until ready to use.

This dressing will keep, refrigerated, for up to 3 days.

# PEANUT SESAME

MAKES 2 CUPS (500 ML)

## INGREDIENTS

- 1 tablespoon sesame oil
- 1 cup (250 ml) smooth peanut butter
- ¾ cup (180 ml) Sweet Sesame Syrup (page 156)
- ¾ cup (180 ml) sunflower oil

## DIRECTIONS

In a blender, combine the sesame oil, peanut butter, and Sweet Sesame Syrup. Blend until smooth, 15 to 20 seconds.

With the blender running on low speed, slowly drizzle in the sunflower oil until the dressing is emulsified and thickened, about 30 seconds. Transfer the dressing to an airtight container and refrigerate until ready to use.

This dressing will keep, refrigerated, for up to 7 days.

# LIME CHILI THAI

### MAKES 2 CUPS (500 ML)

### INGREDIENTS

- 1 cup (250 ml) Sweet Sesame Dressing (page 156)
- Juice from 3 limes (100 ml)
- ¼ cup (60 ml) sambal oelek
- 1 tablespoon fish sauce
- 2 tablespoons agave syrup
- 2 cloves garlic
- 1 teaspoon soy sauce
- 3 tablespoons sunflower oil

### DIRECTIONS

Create a lime chili base: In a blender, combine the lime juice, sambal, fish sauce, agave, garlic, and soy sauce. Process on medium-high speed until smooth and well combined, 20 to 30 seconds. Stop the blender and scrape down the sides of the jar with a spatula as needed.

With the blender running on low speed, slowly drizzle in the sunflower oil until the mixture is emulsified and thickened, about 30 seconds. Transfer the base to an airtight container and refrigerate until ready to make the Lime Chili Thai Dressing.

Combine the base and the Sweet Sesame Dressing in a blender and process until well combined, about 10 seconds. Transfer the dressing to an airtight container and refrigerate until ready to use.

This dressing will keep, refrigerated, for up to 7 days.

# CILANTRO CUMIN

### MAKES 1 CUP (250 ML)

### INGREDIENTS

- 1 clove garlic
- 1 tablespoon coarsely chopped red onion
- ¼ cup (60 ml) apple cider vinegar
- 1 teaspoon lemon juice
- 1 teaspoon Tabasco
- 1 teaspoon ground cumin
- 1 cup packed (40 g) cilantro leaves
- ½ cup (125 ml) olive oil
- ½ teaspoon fine sea salt
- ¼ teaspoon freshly ground black pepper

### DIRECTIONS

In a blender, combine the garlic, onion, vinegar, lemon juice, Tabasco, cumin, and cilantro. Process on medium-high speed until well combined and the cilantro looks coarsely chopped, about 10 seconds. Stop the blender and scrape down the sides of the jar with a spatula as needed.

With the blender running on low speed, slowly drizzle in the olive oil until the dressing is emulsified and thickened, about 30 seconds. Add the salt and pepper, adjusting the seasoning to taste. Transfer the dressing to an airtight container and refrigerate until ready to use.

This dressing will keep, refrigerated, for up to 3 days.

# HONEY CITRUS

MAKES 2 CUPS (500 ML)

## INGREDIENTS

- ¾ cup (180 ml) olive oil
- ⅓ cup + 2 tablespoons (100 ml) honey
- ⅓ cup + 2 tablespoons (100 ml) lemon juice
- ½ cup (125 ml) orange juice
- 1 teaspoon fine sea salt
- ½ teaspoon freshly ground black pepper

## DIRECTIONS

In a blender, combine the olive oil, honey, and lemon and orange juices and process on medium-high speed until combined, 5 to 6 seconds.

Add the salt and pepper, adjusting the seasoning to taste. Transfer the dressing to an airtight container and refrigerate until ready to use.

This dressing will keep, refrigerated, for up to 7 days.

# MAPLE GRAVY

MAKES 2 CUPS (500 ML)

## INGREDIENTS

- 3 tablespoons apple cider vinegar
- 7 teaspoons (35 ml) Quebec maple syrup
- 1 teaspoon minced garlic
- 1 tablespoon whole-grain mustard
- 1½ cups (375 ml) Chicken Gravy (page 124)
- Scant ½ cup (100 ml) olive oil

## DIRECTIONS

In a blender, combine the vinegar, maple syrup, garlic, mustard, and chicken gravy. Blend until smooth, 15 to 20 seconds.

With the blender running on low speed, slowly drizzle in the olive oil until the dressing is emulsified and thickened, about 30 seconds. Transfer the dressing to an airtight container and refrigerate until ready to use.

This dressing will keep, refrigerated, for up to 7 days.

# RED WINE VINNY

MAKES 2 CUPS (500 ML)

## INGREDIENTS

- ⅔ cup (160 ml) red wine vinegar
- 4 cloves garlic
- 1 tablespoon oregano leaves
- ¾ cup (175 ml) store-bought mayonnaise
- ¾ cup (175 ml) olive oil
- 1 teaspoon fine sea salt
- ½ teaspoon freshly ground black pepper

NOTE: BEYOND ITS SOPRANOS SALAD (PAGE 92) APPLICATION, THIS DRESSING IS PERFECT ON ANY SORT OF ITALIAN SUBMARINE SANDWICH (WE'RE LOOKING AT YOU, CAFÉ MILANO IN SAINT-LÉONARD).

## DIRECTIONS

In a blender, combine the vinegar, garlic, oregano, and mayonnaise. Process on medium-high speed until smooth and well combined, 20 to 30 seconds. With the blender running on low speed, slowly drizzle in the olive oil until the mixture is emulsified and thickened, about 30 seconds.

Add the salt and pepper, adjusting the seasoning to taste. Transfer the dressing to an airtight container and refrigerate until ready to use.

This dressing will keep, refrigerated, for up to 7 days.

# HOISIN

MAKES 2 CUPS (500 ML)

## INGREDIENTS

- 1⅓ cups (320 ml) mayonnaise
- 3 tablespoons hoisin sauce
- 2 tablespoons soy sauce
- 3 tablespoons rice vinegar
- 1 tablespoon sesame oil
- 1 tablespoon Hoisin Marinade (page 99)
- 1 teaspoon Chinese five-spice powder
- ½ teaspoon red pepper flakes
- Fine sea salt and freshly ground black pepper

The dressing is made with the same Hoisin Marinade from the Hoisin Duck Salad (page 96), using mayonnaise as a base to give it a smooth, creamy texture. Chinese five-spice powder is added to give depth in flavor with earthy tones from the Szechuan pepper, cinnamon, cloves, fennel, and star anise.

## DIRECTIONS

In a blender, combine all of the ingredients. Process on medium-high speed until smooth and well combined, 15 to 20 seconds. Stop the blender and scrape down the sides of the jar with a spatula as needed. Season to taste with the salt and pepper. Transfer the dressing to an airtight container and refrigerate until ready to use.

This dressing will keep, refrigerated, for up to 7 days.

# BERRY GOOD

MAKES 1 CUP (250 ML)

## INGREDIENTS

- 2 generous tablespoons frozen blueberries
- 2 generous tablespoons frozen raspberries
- 2 generous tablespoons frozen strawberries
- 1 tablespoon agave syrup
- 1 clove garlic
- 3 tablespoons balsamic vinegar
- 7 tablespoons (105 ml) olive oil
- ½ cup (7 g) basil leaves
- ¼ teaspoon fine sea salt
- Pinch of freshly ground black pepper

## DIRECTIONS

In a blender, combine the blueberries, raspberries, strawberries, agave, garlic, and vinegar. Process on medium-high speed until smooth and well combined, 20 to 30 seconds. With the blender running on low speed, slowly drizzle in the olive oil until the mixture is emulsified and thickened, about 30 seconds.

Add the basil, salt, and pepper and blend to combine, 7 to 10 seconds. Stop the blender and scrape down the sides of the jar with a spatula as needed. Adjust the seasoning to taste. Transfer the dressing to an airtight container and refrigerate until ready to use.

This base will keep, refrigerated, for up to 3 days.

# CBD

MAKES 2 CUPS (500 ML)

## INGREDIENTS

- ½ cup (125 ml) apple cider vinegar
- ¼ cup (60 ml) maple syrup
- 1 tablespoon grainy mustard
- 1 garlic clove, minced or pressed
- 1 tablespoon fresh lemon juice
- 1 cup (250 ml) olive oil
- 1 to 2 teaspoons CBD oil
- Fine sea salt and freshly ground black pepper

NOTE: THIS DRESSING IS MEANT FOR OUR LEGALLY BLONDE SALAD (PAGE 102), BUT IF YOU'RE WANTING TO FEEL THE HEALING POWERS OF CBD, YOU CAN USE IT FOR ANY SALAD. IF YOU'RE NEW TO CBD, START WITH 1 TEASPOON IN THIS DRESSING AND SEE HOW YOU FEEL. YOU CAN THEN GRADUALLY WORK YOUR WAY UP TO 2 TEASPOONS, AS DESIRED.

## DIRECTIONS

In a blender, combine the vinegar, maple syrup, mustard, garlic, and lemon juice. Blend until smooth, 10 to 15 seconds.

With the blender running on low speed, slowly drizzle in the olive oil, followed by the CBD oil, until the dressing is emulsified and thickened, about 30 seconds. Season to taste with the salt and pepper. Transfer the dressing to an airtight container and refrigerate until ready to use.

This dressing will keep, refrigerated, for up to 7 days.

# SUN-DRIED TOMATO

MAKES 2 CUPS (500 ML)

## INGREDIENTS

- 2 teaspoons Dijon mustard
- 5 tablespoons (75 ml) Modena balsamic vinegar
- ½ cup (125 ml) water
- 1 tablespoon coarsely chopped red onion
- ¼ cup (6 g) basil leaves
- ½ cup (75 g) sun-dried tomatoes, coarsely chopped
- ¾ cup + 1 tablespoon (190 ml) olive oil
- 1 teaspoon fine sea salt
- ¾ teaspoon freshly ground black pepper

NOTE: WE PREFER TO USE SUN-DRIED TOMATOES THAT ARE PACKED IN OIL. DRAIN THE AMOUNT YOU NEED BEFORE USING THEM IN THIS RECIPE.

## DIRECTIONS

In a blender, combine the mustard, vinegar, water, onion, basil, and sun-dried tomatoes. Process on medium-high speed until smooth and well combined, 20 to 30 seconds. Stop the blender and scrape down the sides of the jar with a spatula as needed.

With the blender running on low speed, slowly drizzle in the olive oil until the dressing is emulsified and thickened, about 30 seconds. Add the salt and pepper, adjusting the seasoning to taste. Transfer the dressing to an airtight container and refrigerate until ready to use.

This dressing will keep, refrigerated, for up to 7 days.

# MINT MADNESS

MAKES 2 CUPS (500 ML)

## INGREDIENTS

- ¼ cup (60 ml) apple cider vinegar
- 2 tablespoons agave syrup
- 1 teaspoon Dijon mustard
- Juice and zest of 1 lime
- 1 garlic clove
- ¼ cup (5 g) mint leaves
- 1 cup (250 ml) olive oil
- 1 teaspoon fine sea salt
- ½ teaspoon freshly ground black pepper

## DIRECTIONS

In a blender, combine the vinegar, agave, mustard, lime zest and juice, garlic, and mint leaves. Process on medium-high speed until smooth and well combined, 15 to 20 seconds. Stop the blender and scrape down the sides of the jar with a spatula as needed.

With the blender running on low speed, slowly drizzle in the olive oil until the dressing is emulsified and thickened, about 30 seconds. Add the salt and pepper, adjusting the seasoning to taste. Transfer the dressing to an airtight container and refrigerate until ready to use.

This dressing will keep, refrigerated, for up to 3 days.

# ENDLESS SUMMER

MAKES 2 CUPS (500 ML)

## INGREDIENTS

- 1 cup (250 ml) Miso Ginger Dressing (page 160)
- 1 cup (250 ml) Tamari Dressing (page 155)

**NOTE: IF YOU'VE MADE THE DRESSINGS BELOW AHEAD OF TIME, YOU MAY NEED TO SHAKE THEM IN THEIR JAR OR GIVE THEM A QUICK SPIN IN A BLENDER TO RE-EMULSIFY THEM BEFORE MEASURING THEM OUT FOR THIS RECIPE.**

## DIRECTIONS

Combine the 2 dressings in a blender and process until well combined, about 10 seconds. Transfer the dressing to an airtight container and refrigerate until ready to use.

This dressing will keep, refrigerated, for up to 7 days.

# CLASSIC BALSAMIC

MAKES 2 CUPS

## INGREDIENTS

- ½ cup (125 ml) balsamic vinegar
- 2 tablespoons honey
- 2 teaspoons Dijon mustard
- 1⅓ cups (325 ml) olive oil
- ¼ teaspoon fine sea salt
- ¼ teaspoon freshly ground black pepper

## DIRECTIONS

In a blender, combine the vinegar, honey, mustard, and olive oil. Process on medium-high speed until smooth and well combined, 5 to 6 seconds. Be careful not to over-blend, as the dressing can become too thick!

Add the salt and pepper, adjusting the seasoning to taste. Transfer the dressing to an airtight container and refrigerate until ready to use.

This dressing will keep, refrigerated, for up to 7 days.

# ÉPICERIE PUMPUI

## MAKES JUST OVER 1 CUP (260 ML)

## INGREDIENTS

- 1 cake of palm sugar
- 7 tablespoons (105 ml) *pla ra*
- 7 tablespoons (105 ml) lime juice
- 7 teaspoons (35 ml) fish sauce

**NOTE: THE PALM SUGAR AND *PLA RA* CAN BOTH BE FOUND IN ASIAN AND THAI GROCERS. *PLA RA* IS A FERMENTED FISH SAUCE ("PRESERVED GOURAMI IN BRINE") AND CAN BE FOUND IN BOTTLED FORM. WE PREFER THE PANTAI NORASINGH BRAND.**

## DIRECTIONS

Melt the palm sugar by placing 1 rock-hard patty in a bowl. Cover with cold water and set aside for 15 minutes to soften slightly. Drain completely. Add 1 teaspoon warm water and cover the bowl with plastic wrap. Microwave for 1 minute. Uncover and stir the melted sugar with a spoon until smooth.

In a small bowl, combine the *pla ra*, lime juice, and fish sauce. Add 4 teaspoons of the melted palm sugar, discarding the rest. Whisk to combine. Refrigerate until ready to use.

This will keep in an airtight container for up to 7 days.

# PESTO

## MAKES 1 CUP (250 ML)

## INGREDIENTS

- ½ cup (7 g) basil leaves
- 1 cup (14 g) flat-leaf parsley leaves
- 1 teaspoon coarsely chopped red onion
- 1 clove garlic
- ¼ cup (20 g) shaved Parmesan
- ⅓ cup (80 ml) olive oil
- ¼ teaspoon fine sea salt
- ¼ teaspoon freshly ground black pepper
- Scant ½ cup (115 ml) Caesar Dressing (page 156)
- 2 teaspoons (10 ml) Smoke Show lightly smoked jalapeño hot sauce

## DIRECTIONS

Create a pesto base: In a blender, combine the basil, parsley, onion, garlic, Parmesan, and olive oil. Process on medium-high speed until smooth and well combined, 20 to 30 seconds. Stop the blender and scrape down the sides of the jar with a spatula as needed. Add the salt and pepper, adjusting the seasoning to taste. Transfer the mixture to an airtight container and refrigerate until ready to make the Pesto Dressing.

Combine the base, the Caesar dressing, and the Smoke Show in a blender and process until well combined, about 10 seconds. Adjust the heat level to taste with the Smoke Show. Transfer the dressing to an airtight container and refrigerate until ready to use.

This dressing will keep, refrigerated, for up to 3 days.

## GINGER WASABI

MAKES 2 CUPS (500 ML)

### INGREDIENTS

- ¼ cup (25 g) coarsely chopped ginger
- 1½ tablespoons wasabi (Japanese horseradish) powder
- 1 teaspoon soy sauce
- 2 tablespoons toasted sesame oil
- 1¼ cups (300 ml) Sweet Sesame Syrup (page 156)
- ½ cup (125 ml) sunflower oil

### DIRECTIONS

In a blender, combine the ginger, wasabi, soy sauce, sesame oil, Sweet Sesame Syrup, and sunflower oil. Process on medium-high speed until smooth and well combined, 20 to 30 seconds. Adjust the seasoning to taste. Transfer the dressing to an airtight container and refrigerate until ready to use.

This dressing will keep, refrigerated, for up to 7 days.

## SPRING DETOX

MAKES 2 CUPS (500 ML)

### INGREDIENTS

- 2 teaspoons Dijon mustard
- 2 tablespoons maple syrup
- 1 clove garlic
- ⅓ cup (80 ml) lemon juice
- ½ cup (125 ml) apple cider vinegar
- 1 cup (250 ml) olive oil
- 1 teaspoon fine sea salt
- ½ teaspoon freshly ground black pepper

### DIRECTIONS

In a blender, combine the mustard, maple syrup, garlic, lemon juice, and vinegar. Process on medium-high speed until smooth and well combined, 5 to 6 seconds.

With the blender running on low speed, slowly drizzle in the olive oil until the dressing is emulsified and thickened, about 30 seconds. Add the salt and pepper, adjusting the seasoning to taste. Transfer the dressing to an airtight container and refrigerate until ready to use.

This dressing will keep, refrigerated, for up to 7 days.

## CREAMY GREEK

MAKES 2 CUPS (500 ML)

### INGREDIENTS

- 1¾ cups (400 ml) plain Mediterranean (10% fat) yogurt
- ¼ cup (60 ml) olive oil
- 2 teaspoons white vinegar
- 4 cloves garlic
- 2 tablespoons oregano leaves
- 1 teaspoon fine sea salt
- ½ teaspoon freshly ground black pepper

### DIRECTIONS

In a blender, combine the yogurt, olive oil, vinegar, garlic, and oregano. Process on medium-high speed until smooth and well combined, 5 to 6 seconds.

Add the salt and pepper, adjusting the seasoning to taste. Transfer the dressing to an airtight container and refrigerate until ready to use.

This dressing will keep, refrigerated, for up to 7 days.

## HONEY MUSTARD

**MAKES 2 CUPS (500 ML)**

### INGREDIENTS

- ¼ cup (60 ml) apple cider vinegar
- 2 tablespoons high-quality balsamic vinegar
- 6 tablespoons (90 ml) honey
- ¼ cup (60 ml) Dijon mustard
- 2 tablespoons water
- Scant 1 cup (235 ml) sunflower oil
- Fine sea salt

### DIRECTIONS

In a blender, combine the vinegars, honey, the mustard, water, and oil. Process on medium-high speed until smooth and well combined, 5 to 6 seconds. Be careful not to over-blend, as the dressing can become too thick! (If that happens, add a little water to loosen.)

Season with salt to taste. Transfer the dressing to an airtight container and refrigerate until ready to use.

This dressing will keep, refrigerated, for up to 7 days.

## CURRIED YOGURT

**MAKES 2 CUPS (500 ML)**

### INGREDIENTS

- 1 cup + 2 tablespoons (280 ml) plain Mediterranean (10% fat) yogurt
- Scant 1 cup (200 ml) mayonnaise
- ⅓ cup (80 ml) mango chutney or honey
- 1 teaspoon mild curry paste or 2 teaspoons curry powder
- 1 garlic clove
- 1 teaspoon Sriracha sauce
- Fine sea salt and freshly ground black pepper

### DIRECTIONS

In a blender, combine the yogurt, mayonnaise, chutney, curry paste, garlic, and Sriracha. Process on medium-high speed until smooth and well combined, 5 to 6 seconds.

Season with salt and pepper to taste. Transfer the dressing to an airtight container and refrigerate until ready to use.

This dressing will keep, refrigerated, for up to 7 days.

## SMOKE SHOW

**MAKES 1 CUP (250 ML)**

### INGREDIENTS

- ½ cup (125 ml) Cilantro Cumin Dressing (page 162)
- ½ cup (125 ml) Caesar Dressing (page 156)
- 2 tablespoons Smoke Show lightly smoked jalapeño hot sauce

**NOTE: IF YOU'VE MADE THE CILANTRO CUMIN DRESSING AHEAD OF TIME, YOU MAY NEED TO SHAKE IT IN ITS JAR OR GIVE IT A QUICK SPIN IN A BLENDER TO RE-EMULSIFY BEFORE MEASURING IT OUT FOR THIS RECIPE.**

### DIRECTIONS

Combine the 2 dressings in a blender and add the Smoke Show sauce. Process until well combined, about 10 seconds. Transfer the dressing to an airtight container and refrigerate until ready to use.

This dressing will keep, refrigerated, for up to 3 days.

# BLUE RANCH

## MAKES 2 CUPS (500 ML)

## INGREDIENTS

- 1 cup (120 g) crumbled blue cheese
- ½ cup (125 ml) sour cream
- ⅓ cup (80 ml) mayonnaise
- 6 tablespoons (90 ml) milk
- 1 tablespoon horseradish cream
- 1½ tablespoons Champagne vinegar
- 1 teaspoon white vinegar
- 1 teaspoon garlic powder
- ½ teaspoon freshly ground black pepper
- ¼ teaspoon fine sea salt

NOTE FROM OUR RECIPE TESTER KENDRA: THIS DRESSING IS THE BOMB! IT'S GOT THE CREAMINESS OF A RANCH DRESSING PLUS THE KICK OF THE BLUE CHEESE WITHOUT BEING OVERLY HEAVY OR CHUNKY!

## DIRECTIONS

In a blender, combine all of the ingredients except the salt and pepper. Process on medium-high speed until smooth and well combined, 15 to 20 seconds. Stop the blender and scrape down the sides of the jar with a spatula as needed.

Add the salt and pepper, adjusting the seasoning to taste. Transfer the dressing to an airtight container and refrigerate until ready to use.

This dressing will keep, refrigerated, for up to 7 days.

# CILANTRO LIME GINGER

## MAKES 1 CUP (250 ML)

## INGREDIENTS

- 1 cup packed cilantro leaves
- 3 tablespoons lime juice
- 3 tablespoons honey or agave syrup
- 3 tablespoons coarsely chopped ginger
- 3 cloves garlic, minced
- ½ cup (125 ml) olive oil
- ½ teaspoon fine sea salt
- ¼ teaspoon freshly ground black pepper

## DIRECTIONS

In a blender, combine the cilantro, lime juice, honey, ginger, and garlic. Blend until coarsely chopped and combined, 15 to 20 seconds.

With the blender running on low speed, slowly drizzle in the olive oil until the dressing is emulsified and thickened, about 30 seconds. Blend in the salt and pepper, adjusting the seasoning to taste. Transfer the dressing to an airtight container and refrigerate until ready to use.

This dressing will keep, refrigerated, for up to 3 days.

Ramen Chicken Peanut Bowl (page 182)

Burrito Bowl (page 192)

Seoul Bowl (page 189)

# Grain Bowls

○ CHAPTER FOUR ○

# Hippie Bowl

◦ SERVES 1 ◦

MANDY | "Roots, rock, reggae," oh yes. This was THE bowl my roommates and I lived on in our university days. Let's hope no photos of my attempted dreadlock-growing days at Mount Royal's drum circle ever surface. Does this bowl blow my mind today like it did back then? Maybe not, but it was my modest beginning with creating grain bowls, so start here as I did, and then work your way up to the Seoul or Pumpui Bowl (pages 189 and 196).

Now that I have four kids, this bowl is still a comfort to make when I'm low on energy and time, which is almost all the time! When we have any leftover grain—jasmine rice, quinoa, brown rice—we reheat it (that is, stir-fry it) and add whatever is hanging around in our fridge and voilà—Hippie Bowl becomes Busy Mom bowl!

## INGREDIENTS

- 1 cup Quinoa (page 201)
- ½ cup Spicy Tofu (page 190)
- ¼ cup canned black beans, drained and rinsed
- ½ cup shredded curly kale
- ¼ cup shredded carrot
- ½ avocado, diced
- 2 tablespoons sunflower seeds

- ⅓ cup Tamari Dressing (page 155)

## DIRECTIONS

Combine all of the ingredients in a large stainless-steel bowl. Top with the dressing, and using tongs, toss until well mixed and dressed.

# Mexi Bowl

∘ SERVES 1 ∘

For those who don't want all the lettuce that comes with our Mexi salad, we've opted for a heartier, more concentrated bowl, highlighting the flavors of our favorite south of the border ingredients. We sell *a lot* of this bowl at our Old Port location, often at dinner time with a glass of crisp wine. We suggest adding the Roasted Chicken Breast (page 149). Oh, and the more cilantro the better . . .

## INGREDIENTS

∘ 1 cup Quinoa (page 201)
∘ ½ cup arugula
∘ ¼ cup diced red bell pepper
∘ ¼ cup canned black beans, drained and rinsed
∘ ¼ cup canned corn kernels, drained and rinsed
∘ ½ avocado, diced
∘ 2 tablespoons sliced red onion
∘ 2 tablespoons pumpkin seeds
∘ 2 tablespoons cilantro leaves

∘ ⅓ cup Cilantro Cumin Dressing (page 162)

## DIRECTIONS

Combine all of the ingredients in a large stainless-steel bowl. Top with the dressing, and using tongs, toss until well mixed and dressed.

# Veggie Power Bowl

◦ SERVES 1 ◦

This is definitely one of our prettiest bowls, packed with so many flavors and textures. Talk about "eating the rainbow," this bowl will fill you up and brighten your spirit. If you want to up the protein ante, add one portion of Roasted Marinated Tofu (page 148) or Tempeh (page 143).

## INGREDIENTS

- 1 cup Quinoa (page 201)
- ½ cup shredded curly kale
- ½ avocado, diced
- ¼ cup canned chickpeas, drained and rinsed
- ¼ cup canned corn kernels, drained and rinsed
- ¼ cup finely sliced red cabbage
- ¼ cup diced red bell pepper
- ¼ cup sliced scallion (green part only)
- ¼ cup cubed feta
- 2 tablespoons cilantro leaves
- 2 tablespoons torn basil leaves

- ⅓ cup Green Power Dressing (page 158)

## DIRECTIONS

Combine all of the ingredients in a large stainless-steel bowl. Top with the dressing, and using tongs, toss until well mixed and dressed.

# Bún Bowl

∘ SERVES 1 ∘

Bún means "noodle" in Vietnamese, and we love to have a gluten-free option, so we decided to riff off the many permutations of a Vietnamese *bún chả*. This bowl is full of naturally gluten-free rice noodles with piles of crunchy veggies, flavorful herbs, and sweetened crispy coconut flakes.

NOTE: WE USE HONEY COCONUT CHIPS, MADE BY BARE SNACKS, IN THIS SALAD, BUT YOU CAN SUBSTITUTE COCONUT FLAKES INSTEAD.

## INGREDIENTS

- 1½ cups Rice Noodles (page 201)
- ¼ cup sliced scallion (green part only)
- ¼ cup diced red bell pepper
- ¼ cup shredded carrot
- ¼ cup thinly sliced red cabbage
- 2 tablespoons toasted unsweetened coconut chips
- 2 tablespoons black and white sesame seeds
- 2 tablespoons torn basil leaves
- 2 tablespoons torn cilantro leaves

- ⅓ cup Endless Summer Dressing (page 166)

## DIRECTIONS

Combine all of the ingredients in a large stainless-steel bowl. Top with the dressing, and using tongs, toss until well mixed and dressed.

## Ramen Chicken Peanut Bowl

◦ SERVES 1 ◦

Reminiscent of the ubiquitous pad Thai, but Mandy's style. This filling, citrusy bowl is packed with texture. It's our mainline Thai-style bowl, with a 2.0 version being the Pumpui Bowl (page 196).

NOTE: FISH SAUCE! DO YOURSELF A FAVOR—DON'T SNIFF THE BOTTLE DIRECTLY (KINDA LIKE NOT LOOKING DIRECTLY AT AN ECLIPSE) BUT DO ADD IT IN THIS RECIPE! IT'S A VERY HARD INGREDIENT TO REPLACE AND IT ADDS A NECESSARY UMAMI DEPTH TO THE WHOLE RECIPE.

## INGREDIENTS

- 1¼ cups Rice Noodles (page 201)
- ¾ cup Shredded Thai Chicken (page 146)
- ½ cup mesclun greens
- ½ cup arugula
- ½ avocado, diced
- ¼ cup thinly sliced red cabbage
- ¼ cup cherry tomatoes, halved
- ¼ cup diced mango
- ¼ cup shredded carrot
- ¼ cup sliced scallion (green part only)
- 2 tablespoons torn mint leaves
- 2 tablespoons torn cilantro leaves
- 2 tablespoons chopped roasted peanuts

- ⅓ cup Lime Chili Thai Dressing (page 162)

## DIRECTIONS

Combine all of the ingredients in a large stainless-steel bowl. Top with the dressing, and using tongs, toss until well mixed and dressed.

## Seoul Bowl

◦ SERVES 1 ◦

Ah, the wonders of kimchi, the delight of pickled marinated cucumber, spicy fried tofu, a crispy fried egg, and spicy mayo. This Seoul Bowl brings together all the essentials in our ode to Korean cuisine.

We will tell you up front: this bowl requires A LOT of prepping of individual components and is quite time consuming. That said, it results in a saucy, luscious, spicy finished product, with plenty of different textures. Also we think that the Mandy's kimchi is more citrus-forward than spicy and fermented, so it's a bit of a gateway kimchi for the uninitiated.

NOTE: THE KIMCHI NEEDS TO BE MADE A MINIMUM OF 24 HOURS AHEAD OF SERVING. PLAN ACCORDINGLY. COMPONENTS THAT SHOULD BE WARMED BEFORE ASSEMBLING THIS BOWL: RICE, QUINOA, TOFU, AND THE FRIED EGG. ALL OF THE COMPONENTS OF THIS BOWL—SPICY MAYO, CRISPY FRIED SHALLOTS, PICKLED CUCUMBER, SPICY TOFU, ETC.— ARE SUPER VERSATILE AND MAKE FANTASTIC ADDITIONS TO YOUR OWN CREATIONS.

## INGREDIENTS

- ½ cup Quinoa (page 201)
- ½ cup Short-Grain Brown Rice (page 201)
- Fine sea salt and freshly ground black pepper
- ½ cup Spicy Tofu (page 189)
- ½ cup Citrus Kimchi (page 191)
- ¼ cup Pickled Cucumber (page 191)
- ½ avocado, sliced
- 2 tablespoons Crispy Fried Shallots (page 151)
- 2 tablespoons black and white sesame seeds
- 2 tablespoons finely chopped nori
- 2 tablespoons Spicy Mayo (page 190)
- 1 egg

## DIRECTIONS

In a bowl, combine the warm quinoa and brown rice. Season to taste with the salt and pepper.

In a large bowl, arrange the ingredients in the following order: the mixed rice and quinoa mixture, the kimchi, the pickled cucumber, the avocado, and the warmed tofu. Then top the bowl with the fried shallots, sesame seeds, chopped nori, and the spicy mayo.

In a frying pan over medium heat, fry an egg sunny-side up. Lay the fried egg on top of the other ingredients in the center of the bowl, and top with the sesame seeds.

# SPICY TOFU

MAKES 2½ CUPS CUBED
TOFU (ABOUT 5 PORTIONS)

## INGREDIENTS

- One 14-ounce (400 g)
  block firm tofu
- 2 tablespoons tamari
- 2 tablespoons togarashi
- 1 tablespoons sesame oil
- 2 tablespoons avocado oil

NOTE: TOGARASHI IS A JAPANESE SPICE BLEND THAT CAN BE FOUND AT SPECIALTY ASIAN GROCERS. YOU CAN APPROXIMATE A VERSION OF IT BY COMBINING ½ TABLESPOON RED PEPPER FLAKES, 1 TEASPOON BLACK AND WHITE SESAME SEEDS, ¼ TEASPOON SZECHUAN PEPPERCORNS, ¼ TEASPOON GROUND GINGER, ¼ TEASPOON POPPY SEEDS, ¼ TEASPOON DRIED ORANGE PEEL, AND ¼ SHEET NORI, CRUMBLED.

## DIRECTIONS

Drain the tofu of any excess liquid. Dice the tofu into ½-inch cubes and transfer to a large bowl.

Combine the tamari, togarashi, and sesame oil with the tofu cubes. Transfer to a ziplock bag or airtight container and refrigerate for a minimum of 2 hours.

Pat the tofu cubes dry with paper towel, then heat the avocado oil in a frying pan over medium heat.

Fry the tofu cubes, stirring regularly, until browned on all sides, 4 to 5 minutes.

The tofu cubes will keep, refrigerated, in an airtight container for up to 5 days.

# SPICY MAYO

MAKES SCANT 1 CUP
(ABOUT 8 PORTIONS)

## INGREDIENTS

- ⅞ cup mayonnaise
- 2 teaspoons Sriracha sauce
- 2 teaspoons tamari
- 1 teaspoon sesame oil

## DIRECTIONS

Combine the mayonnaise, Sriracha, tamari, and sesame oil in a bowl. Stir until completely blended. Transfer to a squeeze bottle or an airtight container and refrigerate until ready to use.

This mayo will keep, refrigerated, for a very long time.

# CITRUS KIMCHI

## MAKES 3 CUPS
(6 PORTIONS)

## INGREDIENTS

- 1¼ pounds napa cabbage
- ⅓ cup minced chives
- ½ cup grapeseed oil or avocado oil
- ⅓ cup freshly squeezed lime juice
- 2 tablespoons agave syrup
- 2 tablespoons Sriracha sauce
- 2 teaspoons tamari
- 1½ teaspoons fine sea salt
- 1 teaspoon red pepper flakes

**NOTE: THIS MAKES A MILD KIMCHI; IF YOU LIKE IT MORE FIERY, INCREASE THE RED PEPPER FLAKES TO 2 TEASPOONS.**

## DIRECTIONS

With a sharp knife, cut the cabbage leaves into small pieces, no larger than 1 inch on a side. You should have about 5 cups of chopped cabbage. Transfer to a large bowl and add the chives.

In a small saucepan, combine the oil, lime juice, agave, Sriracha, tamari, salt, and red pepper flakes. Over medium heat, heat until almost boiling, stirring well to combine. Set aside to cool.

Pour the cooled marinade over the cabbage and chives and mix well. Transfer to a large glass jar or an airtight container and refrigerate for a minimum of 24 hours until ready to use.

The kimchi will keep, refrigerated, for up to 1 week.

# PICKLED CUCUMBER

## MAKES 2 CUPS
(ABOUT 8 PORTIONS)

## INGREDIENTS

- 1 English cucumber, trimmed
- ¼ cup diced red bell pepper
- 2 tablespoons seeded and diced jalapeño (1 small jalapeño)
- ½ cup white vinegar
- ½ cup granulated sugar
- 1 teaspoon fine sea salt

## DIRECTIONS

Slice the cucumber lengthwise. Cut each half into thin half-moon slices.

In a bowl, combine the cucumber, red pepper, and jalapeño.

In a small saucepan, combine the vinegar, sugar, and salt and bring to a boil over medium heat. Stir well to dissolve the sugar, about 30 seconds, then pour the hot liquid into the bowl with the cucumber, pepper, and jalapeño. Let sit until cool.

Transfer to a glass jar or airtight container and refrigerate until ready to use. The pickled cucumber will keep, refrigerated, up to 5 days.

# Burrito Bowl

◦ SERVES 1 ◦

When we came up with this gem, we wanted to deconstruct the typical burrito but keep delicious favorites like rice and beans, shredded chicken (although we use a tofu-based "mock chicken"), ooey-gooey melted cheese, sliced avocados, tortilla chips, and zesty pico de gallo . . . without the heaviness of a flour tortilla. Delicious with a fried or poached egg on top!

## INGREDIENTS

- 2 cups Mexican Rice (page 200)
- ⅓ cup grated cheddar
- ½ cup Pico de Gallo (page 146)
- ½ avocado, sliced
- 2 tablespoons finely chopped cilantro leaves
- 6 to 8 blue corn tortilla chips
- 1 fried egg (optional)

## DIRECTIONS

Warm the Mexican rice in a bowl in the microwave until steaming hot.

Stir in the shredded cheese. Top with the pico de gallo, avocado, cilantro, tortilla chips, and fried egg.

## SERVES 1

Pearl couscous, also known as Israeli couscous, is very underused: so hearty and the perfect size to not interfere or take over the entire bowl. Classic basil pesto flavors combined with a spicy kick from our Smoke Show partners give this take on a classic a super interesting spin. Feel free to splash on some more hot sauce to give your bowl the right amount of fiery kick!

## INGREDIENTS

- 1 cup Pearl Couscous (page 201)
- 1 cup arugula
- ¼ cup diced tomatoes
- ¼ cup diced cucumber
- 2 tablespoons diced red onion
- 2 tablespoons pitted Kalamata olives
- ¼ cup crumbled feta

- ⅓ cup Pesto Dressing (page 168)

## DIRECTIONS

Combine all of the ingredients in a large stainless-steel bowl. Top with the dressing, and using tongs, toss until well mixed and dressed.

## • SERVES 1 •

Épicerie Pumpui is our favorite Thai spot in Montreal. The owners, the two Jesses (Mulder and Massumi), spent years touring Southeast Asia and were inspired by *lan khao gang* (the literal translation is "shop rice curry"). Wanting to collaborate, we co-conspired on this bowl, their take on a *som tam*, also known as: ตำซั่วปุ๋มปุ๋ย.

NOTE: PICKLED MUSTARD LEAVES TEND TO COME IN A VACUUM PACKAGE LABELED AS SOUR
MUSTARD. LOOK FOR THEM, ALONG WITH THE RICE NOODLES, GREEN PAPAYA, DRIED SHRIMP,
THAI CHILIES, YARD-LONG BEANS, AND SAWTOOTH HERB AT A CHINESE OR THAI GROCER.

## INGREDIENTS

- 1 cup Rice Noodles (page 201)
- 1 cup julienned green papaya
- ½ cup sliced pickled mustard leaves
- ½ cup yard-long beans, cut into 1½-inch lengths
- ½ cup halved cherry tomatoes
- ⅓ cup shredded carrot
- 5 cloves garlic, sliced
- 5 stemmed red Thai chilies, minced
- 1 scant tablespoon dried shrimp, soaked in water for 20 minutes before using
- 6 or 7 cooked cocktail shrimp
- ½ cup bean sprouts
- 2 tablespoons coarsely chopped roasted peanuts
- 2 tablespoons sawtooth herb leaves, rolled up and thinly sliced

- 1 cup Épicerie Pumpui Dressing (page 168)

## DIRECTIONS

In a large mixing bowl, combine the noodles, papaya, mustard leaves, yard-long beans, tomatoes, carrot, garlic, chilies, and dried shrimp. Add the dressing. Combine well, using a gloved hand or tongs. Squeeze ingredients here and there to bruise lightly and release the juice of the tomatoes.

Add the cocktail shrimp and bean sprouts. Toss to combine. Serve, garnishing with the toasted peanuts and sawtooth herb leaves.

Dear Mandy, Rebecca, and Meredith,

This bowl is a popular play on *som tam*, the ubiquitous green papaya salad found all over Thailand. This version is more likely to be found in Isan, which is the northeast region of Thailand that borders Laos and Cambodia. The food of the Isan region is known to be funky, pungent, herbaceous, and fiery; therefore, if you have an aversion to spicy food, this salad may not be for you. That being said, it's absolutely delicious, especially on a hot day and it's a wonderful accompaniment to all kinds of grilled meats.

A successful Thai salad should taste sour, salty, savory, funky, and spicy, with an underlying sweetness. Eat this one with accompaniments such as Mandy's roasted chicken, grilled meats, steamed or sticky rice, and a variety of cooked or raw vegetables, such as cucumber, basil sprigs, and raw shoots of morning glory. Or eat it as a meal on its own, reveling in the heat and sweating out memories of your time in the Far East. Feel free to adjust the amount of chilies to your liking. Great with friends and cold beer.

*XO Épicerie Pumpui*

# Caprese Bowl

◦ SERVES 1 ◦

MANDY │ Ina Garten has long been one of our favorite celebrity chefs: her appreciation for full-fat everything and simple ingredients is right up our alley! One of her earlier books features a simple brown rice salad. I've made it so many times at dinner parties, but always add extra Italian deliciousness to it, such as cheese (like good-quality buffalo mozzarella), arugula, and toasted pine nuts. So it's still Barefoot Contessa tasty, but now extra Mandy's tasty.

## INGREDIENTS

- 2 tablespoons olive oil
- 1 cup cherry tomatoes
- 1 cup Short-Grain Brown Rice (page 201)
- ⅓ cup Italian Summer Dressing (page 155)
- 1 cup arugula
- ½ cup shredded buffalo mozzarella
- ¼ cup torn basil leaves
- ¼ cup toasted pine nuts
- Maldon salt and freshly ground black pepper
- Balsamic vinegar

## DIRECTIONS

In a small sauté pan over medium-high heat, warm the olive oil. Sauté the cherry tomatoes whole until they blister and start to pop, about 3 minutes.

Cook the brown rice (or warm it in the microwave to steaming hot if cooked and refrigerated). In a large stainless-steel bowl, combine the rice with the dressing until well coated and absorbed. Top with the arugula, mozzarella, basil, and pine nuts and toss well to combine. Season with Maldon salt, pepper, and a splash or two of olive oil and balsamic vinegar, as needed.

# GRAIN BASES

## MEXICAN RICE

MAKES 12 CUPS
(6 PORTIONS)

### INGREDIENTS

- 3 tablespoons avocado oil
- ½ onion, diced small
- ⅓ cup minced garlic
- 2 tablespoons cumin
- 2 teaspoons red pepper flakes
- 2 cups dry short-grain brown rice
- One 28-ounce can (2 cups) diced tomatoes, strained
- 4 cups low-sodium vegetable broth
- 2 cups Mock Chicken (page 142)
- 1¼ cups canned black beans, drained and rinsed
- 1¼ cups canned corn kernels, drained and rinsed
- Fine sea salt and freshly ground black pepper

NOTE: IT'S TOO AWKWARD TO MAKE ONE SERVING OF THIS, SO IT'S BEST MADE AS A LARGE BATCH, TO FEED A GROUP OR ONE PERSON ALL WEEK!

### DIRECTIONS

In a large Dutch oven or heavy-bottomed pot, warm the oil over medium-low heat. Stir in the onion, garlic, cumin, and pepper flakes and fry until fragrant and translucent, about 5 minutes. Add the rice, followed by the strained tomatoes, vegetable broth, mock chicken, beans, and corn. Stir well.

Bring to a boil over medium-high heat, then cover, lower to a simmer and cook for 1 hour, giving the contents of the pot a good stir every 15 or 20 minutes.

Remove from the heat, season to taste with the salt and pepper, and serve immediately if feeding a group. Otherwise, set aside to cool, then transfer to an airtight container and refrigerate until ready to use.

Mexican Rice will keep, refrigerated, for up to 1 week.

## DRESSED FARRO

MAKES 3 CUPS

### INGREDIENTS

- 1½ cups pearled dry farro
- 2 cups apple cider
- 1 cup water
- 2 bay leaves
- 1 teaspoon fine sea salt
- ½ teaspoon freshly ground black pepper
- ⅓ cup lemon juice
- ⅔ cup olive oil

### DIRECTIONS

In a large saucepan, bring the farro, apple cider, and water to a boil. Stir in the bay leaves and salt and pepper. Cook over medium heat for 30 minutes until the farro is tender (it will still have some bite). Drain the farro, discarding the bay leaves, then return to the pot and stir in the lemon juice and olive oil and adjust seasoning to taste with more salt and pepper. Let cool and then refrigerate until ready to use.

The cooked farro will keep, refrigerated, in an airtight container for up to 1 week.

# QUINOA (OR RED QUINOA)

**MAKES 3 CUPS
(4 TO 6 PORTIONS)**

### INGREDIENTS

- 1⅔ cups water
- 1 cup dry quinoa (or red quinoa)

### DIRECTIONS

In a heavy-bottomed saucepan, bring the water to a boil over medium-high heat. Stir in the quinoa, and when the water returns to a boil, lower the heat, cover, and simmer for 15 minutes. Remove from the heat and keep covered a further 5 minutes. Fluff the quinoa with a fork.

Cooked quinoa will keep, refrigerated, in an airtight container for up to 1 week.

# SHORT-GRAIN BROWN RICE

**MAKES 3 CUPS
(4 TO 6 PORTIONS)**

### INGREDIENTS

- 1 cup dry short-grain brown rice
- 1¾ cups water
- 1 tablespoon unsalted butter

### DIRECTIONS

In a heavy-bottomed saucepan, combine the rice with the water and butter. Bring to a boil over medium-high heat. Cover, turn the heat to the lowest setting, and simmer for 45 minutes. Remove from the heat and keep covered a further 15 minutes. Fluff the rice with a fork.

Cooked brown rice will keep, refrigerated, in an airtight container for up to 1 week.

# PEARL COUSCOUS

**MAKES 6 CUPS
(6 PORTIONS)**

### INGREDIENTS

- 2½ cups water
- 2 cups pearl couscous
- 2 tablespoons olive oil

### DIRECTIONS

In a heavy-bottomed saucepan, bring the water to a boil over medium-high heat. Stir in the couscous and the olive oil. When the water returns to a boil, lower the heat almost completely, cover, and simmer for 10 minutes. Remove from the heat and keep covered a further 5 minutes. Fluff the couscous with a fork.

Cooked couscous will keep, refrigerated, in an airtight container for up to 1 week.

# RICE NOODLES

**MAKES 6 CUPS
(12 PORTIONS)**

### INGREDIENTS

- One 8.8-ounce (250 g) package thin rice noodles
- Sesame oil, as needed

### DIRECTIONS

Place the rice noodles in a large mixing bowl.

Bring 8 cups water to a boil, then pour over the rice noodles and cover completely.

Stir the noodles every minute or so to loosen. When they look and feel limp and tender, about 3 to 4 minutes, drain them and run them under cold water. Drain again and toss with a splash of sesame oil to keep the noodles from sticking to each other.

These will keep, refrigerated, for up to 5 days.

Coconut Chocolate Tarter (page 212)

# Sweets

◦ CHAPTER FIVE ◦

# MANDY'S CHOCOLATE CHIP COOKIES

### Makes 12 large cookies

These cookies were the impetus for founding Mandy's (see "Our Story," page 1). And this recipe right here has also been the most requested bit of Mandy's intel over the last decade: something we've held on to really tightly . . . until now. With such a huge volume to make, we select cookie makers and bakers at only one-third of our locations, and from there we distribute the additional dough to the other locations to bake on-site.

MANDY | The genesis story? When I was 10, I remember making chocolate chip cookies with my mom at our cottage up north in the Laurentians. I don't know what I liked more—the crispy edges and the oozing-with-melted-chocolate centers of the baked cookies or just licking the batter off the spoon, tasting the buttery salty-sweet dough, and feeling at one with everyone and everything. Over the years, I kept making the cookies, tweaking the recipe to give the cookies the best flavor possible . . . and these are irresistible.

NOTE: ANY LEFTOVER COOKIES (HAHAHAHA) CAN BE USED IN COCONUT CHOCOLATE TRUFFLES (PAGE 212). BEFORE YOU START THIS RECIPE, HAVE THE EGG SITTING OUT AT ROOM TEMPERATURE BUT THE CHOCOLATE CHIPS CHILLED IN THE REFRIGERATOR.

## YOU WILL NEED

- Parchment-lined
  18- × 13-inch sheet tray
- 2-ounce (large) cookie
  scoop (optional)

## INGREDIENTS

- ½ cup packed (110 g)
  brown sugar
- ¼ cup (50 g) granulated sugar
- 2 teaspoons Maldon salt
- ½ cup + 2 tablespoons (140 g)
  cultured unsalted butter, cubed
  (we like L'Ancêtre brand)
- 1 large egg, at room temperature
- ½ teaspoon baking soda
- 2 teaspoons pure vanilla extract
- 1¼ cups (170 g) all-purpose flour
- 1 cup (185 g) dark chocolate
  chips, chilled (see Note)

## DIRECTIONS

Preheat the oven to 375°F.

In a large bowl, whisk the brown sugar, granulated sugar, and salt to combine.

In a small saucepan, over medium heat, melt the butter. Whisking gently and consistently, keep cooking the butter as it foams. Remove from the heat when the foam begins to subside and the butter starts to brown and smell nutty, about 6 minutes total. Pour the butter into the bowl with the sugars then whisk to combine well. Set aside to cool to room temperature, about 5 to 10 minutes.

Once the butter and sugar mixture feels lukewarm, whisk in the egg, followed by the baking soda and vanilla extract until fully incorporated.

Next, use a spatula or wooden spoon to stir in the flour until well combined. The consistency should be thick but spoon-able; if it feels too runny, refrigerate for 15 to 30 minutes or so to firm it up.

Use a spatula to stir in the chocolate chips, making sure they are well distributed throughout.

Scoop or spoon 12 balls of batter (about 2 ounces/60 g each) onto the parchment-lined sheet tray (the batter will spread out as it bakes), laying out 3 rows of 4 cookies.

Bake until golden and semi-firm around the edges, but still very soft in the center, about 12 to 13 minutes. Remove from the oven and let cool on the tray for a few minutes before transferring to a wire rack to cool completely. These will keep in an airtight container for several days.

# GLUTEN-FREE SCONE "CLOUDS"

Makes 15 cookies

Through the years of friends and family loving our classic chocolate chip cookies, we've always had the dear friend or colleague who has celiac disease or a gluten intolerance. One day we said, "Enough is enough. Let's make something just as delicious for them!" Even our fussy gluten-loving kids enjoy these fluffy "clouds" of a cookie—so light and airy that they turn out more like a scone than a cookie. It's always fun when a good intention turns into a happy culinary surprise!

## YOU WILL NEED

○ Parchment-lined 18- × 13-inch sheet tray

## INGREDIENTS

○ 3 tablespoons coconut oil, melted and cooled
○ 1 tablespoon vanilla extract
○ ¼ cup (60 ml) maple syrup
○ 1 large egg
○ 1½ cups (150 g) almond meal or almond flour
○ ¼ teaspoon fine sea salt
○ 2 tablespoons coconut flour
○ ½ cup (90 g) dark chocolate chips
○ ½ cup (60 g) unsweetened shredded coconut (optional, definitely adds to the "cloud" fluff)

## DIRECTIONS

Preheat the oven to 350°F.

In a large bowl, combine the coconut oil, vanilla extract, maple syrup, and egg, and whisk until combined.

Stir in the almond meal, salt, and coconut flour and mix until smooth.

Using a spatula or wooden spoon, fold in the chocolate chips and shredded coconut, if using, until evenly distributed.

Use a small cookie scoop or 1 heaped tablespoon to portion out the cookies—and transfer each semi-sphere to a sheet tray lined with parchment. The batter doesn't spread much during cooking, so you can place the cookies fairly close together.

Bake for 12 to 15 minutes, until the cookies begin to brown around the edges, but are still golden overall.

# COCONUT CHOCOLATE TRUFFLES

Makes 40 to 45 truffles

This one goes out to those who are severely—and desperately—addicted to chocolate. When we were trying out our flourless Chocolate Bombz (page 225) for guest consumption, one of our kitchen managers, Alfonso Barba (who manages our Crescent kitchen), started rolling them out, adding our cookie batter to them and then dusting them in coconut flakes. He was either a genius or a high-calorie devil! We know the allure of a deeply dense and fudgy half-baked chocolate dessert, oh yes. And so here we combined all of our favorite indulgent components into these heavenly balls. Yep, they truly are balls of heaven. Each one has crumbled Mandy's chocolate chip cookies packed into ooey gooey brownie-esque chocolate, and to finish it off, they are rolled in toasted coconut flakes.

NOTE: THESE TRUFFLES CONTAIN RAW EGGS.

## YOU WILL NEED

- Food processor (optional)
- 18- x 13-inch sheet tray
- Digital scale (optional, but ideal for making very evenly sized truffles)

## INGREDIENTS

- 7 ounces (200 g) Mandy's Chocolate Chip Cookies (page 206), about 4 cookies
- 2 cups (150 g) unsweetened shredded coconut
- 1½ pounds (700 g) Chocolate Bombz batter (page 225), 1 batch
- 2 tablespoons vanilla extract

## DIRECTIONS

Preheat the oven to 350°F.

Manually break up the cookies into the bowl of a stand mixer until coarsely crumbled (or pulse in a food processor a few times).

Spread the coconut flakes onto a sheet tray and bake for 5 minutes or so until fragrant and lightly golden in color. Stir the flakes and allow to cool on the tray before transferring to a shallow bowl or small tray.

Make one batch of Chocolate Bombz batter. Stir it into the chocolate chip cookie crumbs, then stir in the vanilla extract.

Mix on the lowest speed for 2 minutes until the crumbs are completely distributed throughout the batter.

Refrigerate until set, at least 1 hour.

Use a small spoon to scoop out a 20 g portion (equivalent to a heaped teaspoon, though a regular teaspoon will work better than a measuring teaspoon). Use your hands to roll the dough into a ball and then place the balls on a parchment-lined tray. You may wish to rinse and wet your hands every few truffles to make the rolling less messy.

When you've finished rolling all the truffles, roll each truffle in the coconut flakes to coat. Transfer to an airtight container (you can separate layers of truffles with parchment paper) and refrigerate until ready to serve. Let sit at room temperature for 15 minutes before enjoying; the truffles will continue to be good over the next 2 hours.

# SALTED PECAN SHORTBREAD SQUARES

Makes 16 2-inch squares

We adore pecan pie. Well, actually, our first love was Québecois tarte au sucre—sugar pie. On the way up to our family cottage every Friday night, we would always stop at this roadside stand on Route 117, north of Sainte-Agathe-des-Monts, to pick up a sugar pie (as the family grew, it got to be three sugar pies). Then, later in life, we discovered pecan pie, essentially pecans in a sugar pie, and, were even more hooked. This version is easy to eat on the go, with these bite-size mini squares . . . They're addictive. Enjoy!

## YOU WILL NEED

- 9-inch square cake pan
- Nonstick cooking spray or softened unsalted butter, for greasing

## INGREDIENTS

### CRUST

- ¾ cup (110 g) all-purpose flour
- ¼ cup (40 g) cornstarch
- ½ cup (75 g) confectioners' sugar
- 1 teaspoon fine sea salt
- ½ cup (113 g) cold unsalted butter, cubed

### FILLING

- ¾ cup (170 g) unsalted butter
- ½ cup (100 g) brown sugar
- 3 tablespoons agave syrup
- ½ teaspoon vanilla extract
- ½ teaspoon Maldon salt, and more for sprinkling
- 2 tablespoons heavy cream
- 3 cups (375 g) coarsely chopped pecans

## DIRECTIONS

To make the crust, cover a 9-inch square baking pan with heavy-duty aluminum foil. Push the foil neatly into the corners and up the sides of the pan, using 2 pieces to make sure the foil overlaps all edges (the overhang will help you remove the square from the pan after baking). Grease the foiled pan with nonstick cooking spray or softened butter.

In the bowl of a food processor fitted with the blade attachment, combine the flour, cornstarch, sugar, and salt. Pulse a few times to mix. Add the butter and pulse until the mixture resembles coarse sand with a few pea-size clumps of butter, about 6 or 7 pulses. The mixture will seem sandy and dry—that's okay. Pour it into the prepared cake pan and, using your hands or an offset spatula, spread it out into an even layer, pressing down firmly with your palms or fingers to compress. Refrigerate for 15 minutes.

Preheat the oven to 350°F.

Bake the crust until it looks set—it will be soft to the touch, but set as it cools—and not browned, 15 to 17 minutes. Set on a rack to cool, leaving the oven on.

To make the filling, in a heavy saucepan over medium-low heat, combine the butter, brown sugar, agave, vanilla extract, and salt. Stir with a wooden spoon until the sugar dissolves. Increase the heat to medium and bring the mixture to a boil, then lower the heat and simmer gently for 3 minutes. Remove from the heat and stir in the cream and chopped pecans until well combined.

Pour the pecan mixture over the crust (it's okay if the crust is still warm). Bake until the filling is bubbling and caramel-colored, 17 to 20 minutes. Cool completely on a rack and sprinkle with Maldon salt to your taste.

Use the foil overhang to lift the baked square out of the pan and onto a cutting board. Cut into 2-inch squares. Serve at room temperature. If you're having trouble cutting through evenly, refrigerate for a few hours and then use your sharpest chef's knife to slice perfect squares.

The squares can be stored in an airtight container for up to 5 days, using parchment paper between layers. They can also be wrapped tightly and frozen for up to 3 months—thaw overnight before serving.

# PALEO
## BANANA BREAD
### Serves 6 to 8

MANDY | *This is not a treat that's on offer at Mandy's—rather it is more of a peek behind the scenes, as it's something I bake often for our staff meetings. The best way to deal with browning bananas, this is a family recipe that I've tweaked to give it a Paleo feel. (Of course the chocolate chips make it not so Paleo, but I had to have something crave-worthy in there!)*

*This banana bread will surprise you by being neither flat nor dense (as often ends up being the case with many gluten-free baked goods): in fact it's really moist and flavorful. Of course, because it is gluten-free, it is crumblier than "regular" banana bread, so it's best enjoyed on a plate with a fork . . .*

## YOU WILL NEED

- 8- × 4-inch (1-pound) loaf pan
- Nonstick cooking spray

## INGREDIENTS

- 3 medium ripe bananas, mashed
- ¼ cup (65 g) almond butter
- 1 teaspoon vanilla extract
- 2 large eggs, at room temperature
- ½ cup (65 g) coconut flour
- 1 teaspoon baking soda
- ½ teaspoon cinnamon
- ¼ teaspoon fine sea salt
- ½ cup (90 g) dark chocolate chips, plus extra for sprinkling
- ½ cup (60 g) toasted pecans, plus extra for sprinkling
- ½ cup (30 g) toasted unsweetened coconut flakes
- 1 banana (optional)

## DIRECTIONS

Preheat the oven to 350°F. Spray the loaf pan with cooking spray and set aside.

In a large bowl, combine the mashed bananas, almond butter, and vanilla extract. Whisk to combine into a smooth and creamy mixture.

Whisk in the eggs, one at a time.

Stir in the coconut flour, baking soda, cinnamon, and salt; mix again until just combined. Gently fold in the chocolate chips, pecans, and coconut flakes.

Pour the batter into the prepared loaf pan, smoothing the top with a spatula. Sprinkle some additional chocolate chips and pecans over top. If you feel like getting real fancy decoration-wise (and you have an extra banana), slice a banana down the center and lay the two long vertical banana halves on the top of the bread before baking.

Bake for about 30 minutes, until golden brown around the edges and a tester inserted into the center comes out clean (it may be chocolaty!).

Transfer to a rack to cool completely before unmolding and slicing to serve.

# JOODLES'S APPLE CRISP

*Serves 6*

MANDY | *Our dad used to call our mom Judy, "Joodles." Even though he passed away suddenly in 2012, the Joodles nickname lives on with her grandkids, who have all taken to calling her by the same pet name. I can still vividly picture the white ceramic casserole she would make her apple crisp in, and the smell of caramelizing sugar, cinnamon, and nutmeg. She made it so effortlessly, and it was always delicious. This is best served warm, with, of course, vanilla ice cream.*

NOTE: YOU CAN EXPERIMENT WITH ANY NUMBER OF APPLE VARIETIES, AND YOU'RE WELCOME TO SLICE YOUR APPLES. WE LIKE OURS CHOPPED.

## YOU WILL NEED

- 8- × 8-inch baking dish

## INGREDIENTS

- 6 McIntosh or Golden Delicious apples, peeled, cored, and chopped
- 2 tablespoons granulated sugar
- 1¾ teaspoons ground cinnamon, divided
- 1 teaspoon ground nutmeg
- 1½ teaspoons lemon juice
- ¾ cup (75 g) old-fashioned oats
- ¾ cup (160 g) all-purpose flour
- 1 cup (215 g) light brown sugar
- ¾ cup (170 g) cold salted butter, diced into small cubes, plus more for greasing the baking dish
- Pinch of Maldon salt

## DIRECTIONS

Preheat the oven to 350°F. Butter your baking dish and set aside.

In a large bowl, combine the apples, granulated sugar, ¾ teaspoon of cinnamon, nutmeg, and lemon juice. Stir to combine, then transfer to the prepared baking dish.

In a separate bowl, combine the oats, flour, and brown sugar until well mixed. Stir in the cubes of butter and a pinch of salt, and use your hands or a pastry blender to blend the butter into the dry mixture until the mixture feels sandy, with a few pea-size clumps left in for good measure.

Distribute the oat topping and remaining cinnamon over the apples, and gently pat to even it all out. Bake for 45 minutes until the dish is fragrant, you can see the apples bubbling, and the topping is a nice golden-brown color.

Serve in the bowls or mugs of your choice, with ice cream!

# LEMON-ORANGE BUTTERCREAM COOKIES

### Makes 35 to 40 sandwich cookies

We loved serving these at smaller events when the restaurants used to close for private parties such as close friends' bridal or baby showers. There's something equally dainty and seasonal to these buttery citrusy shortbread cookies. Enjoy with a pot of your favorite tea; we adore Twinings Earl Grey.

NOTE: THE DOUGH FOR THE COOKIES NEEDS TO BE COMPLETELY CHILLED BEFORE BAKING AND IS BEST REFRIGERATED OVERNIGHT. PLAN ACCORDINGLY.

## YOU WILL NEED

- 2 parchment-lined 18- x 13- inch sheet trays

## INGREDIENTS

### COOKIES

- ¾ cup (170 g) unsalted butter, softened
- ½ cup (100 g) granulated sugar
- 1 large egg yolk
- ½ teaspoon vanilla extract
- 2 cups (240 g) all-purpose flour
- ¼ cup (30 g) slivered almonds

### LEMON-ORANGE FILLING

- 3 tablespoons unsalted butter, softened
- 1½ tablespoons lemon juice
- 1 teaspoon grated orange zest
- 1 cup (115 g) confectioners' sugar

## DIRECTIONS

To make the cookies, use a stand mixer fitted with the paddle attachment, on medium speed, to cream the butter and sugar until light and fluffy, about 2 minutes. Add the egg yolk and the vanilla extract, stopping the machine and using a spatula to scrape down the sides and the bottom of the bowl.

With the mixer on low speed, gradually add the flour and mix until well combined.

Lay a square of plastic wrap on the counter. Place half of the cookie batter on the plastic wrap and use the wrap to shape the dough into a 10-inch-long log (about 1½ inches in diameter). Repeat with the remaining half of the dough to shape a second log. Wrap both logs tightly and refrigerate overnight.

Preheat the oven to 400°F.

The next day, unwrap each log and use a sharp knife to trim the ends. Cut each log into ¼-inch-thick even slices. Transfer the slices onto 2 parchment-lined large sheet trays, keeping about 1 inch between each disk. Sprinkle half of the cookies (one trayful) with the slivered almonds, pressing them down lightly into the dough to help them stick.

Bake one tray at a time for 8 to 10 minutes, until the cookies are golden brown around the edges. Set aside to cool while you prepare the filling.

To make the filling, in a small bowl, cream the butter, lemon juice, and orange zest until fluffy. Gradually stir in the confectioners' sugar until smooth.

Assemble the cookies: using a small spatula or regular spoon, spread approximately half a teaspoon of filling on the bottom of a plain cookie, then top the filling with an almond cookie. Press gently together. Repeat with the remaining cookies.

The cookies will keep at room temperature in an airtight container for up to 5 days.

# CHOCOLATE BOMBZ

*Makes 12 muffin-size bombz*

MANDY | *There has yet to be a dinner I host or get invited to where these flourless Chocolate Bombz are not a show-stopping, scene-stealing, crowd-pleasing sensation. Rich and fudgy but gluten-free, this dense chocolate party in your mouth is about to get real! These are a versatile treat, as you can turn them into a plated dessert: We like to serve them with fresh berries and Caramel Sauce (see below). You can also bake the batter as a whole cake; just be sure to cook it a little longer: 35 to 40 minutes or until an inserted knife comes out clean.*

## YOU WILL NEED

- 12-cup muffin tray (or an 8-inch springform pan if you're making the cake), greased with unsalted butter or nonstick cooking spray

## INGREDIENTS

- ⅔ cup (150 g) salted butter, cut into pieces
- 1 cup (180 g) dark chocolate chips
- ¾ cup (170 g) granulated sugar
- ⅔ cup (65 g) unsweetened cocoa powder, sifted
- 4 large eggs
- Optional: 1 cup of washed seasonal fresh berries (such as strawberries, blueberries, raspberries, or blackberries)

## DIRECTIONS

Preheat the oven to 350°F.

In a small saucepan over low heat, melt the butter and chocolate chips, stirring until smooth and blended. Remove from the heat.

Combine the sugar and cocoa in the bowl of a stand mixer with the whisk attachment. Add the eggs, whisking at low speed for 1 minute until blended.

With the mixer still running, pour in the warm chocolate-butter mixture and continue whisking for about 1 minute, until smooth.

Spoon the batter into the muffin tray, filling each cavity about ⅔ full. Bake until a tester inserted into the center comes out clean, 23 to 25 minutes.

Allow the cakes to cool completely on a rack. Then use an offset spatula or a butter knife to gently unmold them—because they are gluten-free, they are a little more fragile than an average muffin.

These mini cakes can be made 1 day ahead—keep them in the tray, covered in plastic, and refrigerate. Warm the cakes in a 350°F oven for 10 minutes before serving.

# CARAMEL SAUCE

MAKES 500 ML
(2 CUPS) SAUCE

## INGREDIENTS

- 1½ cups (300 g) granulated sugar
- ¼ cup (60 ml) water
- 1½ teaspoons lemon juice
- 1 cup (250 ml) heavy cream
- ¼ stick (2 tablespoons) unsalted butter
- 1 tablespoon Maldon salt

## DIRECTIONS

In a heavy saucepan over low heat, gently stir the sugar, water, and lemon juice until the sugar is completely dissolved.

Increase the heat to medium-high and boil the syrup, without stirring it, until it takes on a deep amber color, 7 to 8 minutes. Remove from the heat.

Slowly pour in the cream (the liquid will bubble vigorously) while whisking vigorously but carefully to incorporate. If some of the caramel seizes up, return the saucepan to low heat, stirring until any remaining caramel pieces dissolve.

Add the butter and salt and whisk until smooth. Serve warm or at room temperature.

This sauce can be made ahead, stored in a jar, and refrigerated for up to 7 days. (Warm it in a microwave or over low heat to loosen before serving.)

# NANA'S SHORTBREAD COOKIES

*Makes 48 2-inch cookies*

*Every holiday season, as much as we would look forward to the crooner hits our parents would play on the tape deck and the turkey our mom would roast with all the fixings (she converted to Judaism when she fell in love with our dad, but that didn't stop the turkey at Hanukkah!), nothing felt as delicious or traditional as our Nana's shortbread cookies. We still have her jar of cookie cutters: a candy cane, a star, a Christmas tree (my favorite as it was the biggest), little snowmen . . . After she took the cookies out of the oven, she would sprinkle them with tinsel-colored sanding sugar, making them shine like fresh snowflakes on Christmas Eve . . . They were and still are like magic to us.*

**NOTE: THE RECIPE YIELD WILL VARY BASED ON THE SIZE OF YOUR THEMED COOKIE CUTTERS.**

## YOU WILL NEED

- Cookie cutters of your choice
- 2 parchment-lined 18- × 13-inch sheet trays

## INGREDIENTS

- 1 cup (225 g) salted butter, at room temperature
- ½ cup (100 g) light brown sugar
- 1 teaspoon vanilla extract
- 2 cups (250 g) all-purpose flour, plus more for rolling out the dough
- Sanding sugar or raw sugar, for dusting (optional), or sprinkles of any and all colors and shapes for festive times of the year!

## DIRECTIONS

Preheat the oven to 350°F.

In a large bowl, working by hand with a wooden spoon (in honor of Nana), soften the butter until creamy, then stir in the sugar and mix really well, then stir in the vanilla extract.

Add the flour, one cup at a time, kneading the mixture thoroughly—don't be afraid to use your hands here to achieve a homogeneous dough.

Wrap the dough in plastic and refrigerate for 30 minutes or longer.

On a counter dusted with flour, roll the dough out until it's about ⅛ inch thick. Cut out shapes with the cookie cutters of your choice and transfer as many as you can fit to each sheet tray. We can fit 24 round cookies on one tray, as they don't spread and so need only a little space around them. Knead the dough scraps together, re-roll and make a few more final cookies.

Sprinkle with the sanding sugar of your choice.

Bake one tray at a time until the edges of the cookies start to be golden brown, 13 to 15 minutes, then use a flat spatula to transfer to a rack to cool.

These can be stored in an airtight container for up to 5 days, using parchment paper to separate the layers.

# MINI KEY LIME PIES

Makes 6 muffin-size mini pies;
also works well in 6 individual ramekins

Some of our happiest Wolfe Pack family memories are evenings in South Florida, stuffing our faces with key lime pies as the sun went down. While writing this book, we were experimenting with converting that pitch perfect summer recipe from "makes one dozen" to many multiples of that in order to serve all of our Montreal locations for summer. Fresh lime zest and juice are key!

## YOU WILL NEED

- 6-cup muffin tray
- channel knife

## INGREDIENTS

- 2½ tablespoons grated lime zest
- 4 egg yolks
- 14-ounce (396 g) can sweetened condensed milk
- ½ cup (125 ml) lime juice
- 1½ cups (210 g) crushed graham crackers
- 3 tablespoons granulated sugar
- 5 tablespoons (70 g) melted unsalted butter
- ¾ cup (180 ml) heavy cream
- ¼ cup (30 g) confectioners' sugar

## DIRECTIONS

Preheat the oven to 325°F.

Start by making the filling. In a large bowl, combine 1½ tablespoons of the lime zest with the egg yolks, whisking well until the mixture is pale green, about 2 minutes. Whisk in the condensed milk, followed by the lime juice, and set the bowl aside at room temperature to allow the mixture to thicken.

In a separate bowl, combine the graham cracker crumbs, granulated sugar, and butter, stirring to mix thoroughly. Use your hands to fill 6 cups of a muffin pan, pressing with your fingers to spread the crumb crust around evenly.

Bake for 8 minutes or until golden brown. Let cool for 15 minutes.

Pour the filling into the crusts and then bake the mini pies until the mixture jiggles slightly, about 15 to 17 minutes. Set aside to cool at room temperature, then cover and refrigerate until chilled, 2 to 3 hours.

In a large bowl or the bowl of a stand mixer fitted with the whisk attachment, whip the cream, slowly adding the sugar. Once partially whipped, add the remaining tablespoon of lime zest, then whip the cream to firm peaks. Spoon dollops of whipped cream over the top of the 6 mini pies.

Feel free to use a channel knife to prepare dainty strips of lime zest. Curl the strips and add them to the tops of the mini key lime pies.

# NUT BUTTER AND CHOCOLATE CUPS

### Makes 9 mini cups

These are like a homemade Reese's peanut butter cup, and can be made more healthy by using chocolate with a high percentage of cocoa solids, e.g., 85%. There are so many reasons we love this recipe: it involves NO COOKING OR BAKING (it's a freezer that does the trick); it's versatile (works well with peanut butter, almond butter, or cashew butter); and if you want, you can easily double this recipe to make 18 mini cups. One time we made these (when our freezer was busted) on a January afternoon when it was −23°C outside. Good old Canadian Mother Nature froze everything reeeeal quick!

NOTE: THE JAM ADDITION IS OPTIONAL. WE LIKE BONNE MAMAN CHERRY OR RASPBERRY, BUT YOU CAN USE ANY FLAVOR YOU WANT.

## YOU WILL NEED

- Mini cupcake or muffin pan, greased with unsalted butter or nonstick cooking spray

## INGREDIENTS

- 5 ounces (150 g) dark chocolate, divided
- ½ cup (125 g) smooth unsweetened nut butter of your choice
- 2 teaspoons maple syrup
- 2 teaspoons coconut flour
- Pinch of fine sea salt (if your nut butter is unsalted)
- ½ cup (170 g) jam of your choice (optional)
- Maldon salt, for sprinkling

## DIRECTIONS

Cut half of the chocolate into small pieces and melt it in a small bowl in the microwave, working in bursts of 15 seconds. Stir well until completely smooth.

Add two (overflowing!) teaspoons of melted chocolate to the bottoms of 9 cups. Use the back of the spoon to spread the chocolate all the way up the sides of each cup.

Place the pan in the freezer for at least 15 minutes to harden the chocolate.

In a bowl, combine the nut butter, maple syrup, coconut flour, and salt and stir until well mixed and smooth. Spoon 1 teaspoon of the mixture into each chocolate cup, leaving a little room at the top. Add a small dollop of jam, if using.

Cut the remaining chocolate into pieces and melt it in a small bowl in the microwave, working in bursts of 15 seconds. Stir well until completely smooth.

Spoon 2 teaspoons of warm chocolate over the top of the nut butter (and jam), then use an offset spatula to spread the chocolate evenly, covering all the filling. Sprinkle with salt as desired. Freeze for 5 to 10 minutes until the chocolate top has solidified. Unmold and serve!

These cups will keep, refrigerated, in an airtight container, for up to 3 weeks.

# Acknowledgments

MANDY

This has truly been a labor of love, and when you love what you do, you never work a day in your life, right? This journey would not have been possible without these special souls for whom I am immeasurably grateful:

To Meredith, Kendra, Lindsay, Robert, and the Penguin Random House Canada team, thank you for making this a smooth process. I can't wait for more collaborations! To Allison and Kerrie, the photographer and stylist with the best smiles, attitudes, and Irish and British accents: your vision is our vision. Thank you for capturing what delights our eyes as well. To Sarah Lazar, our original graphics queen, you have been on this wonderful ride for most of it, always infusing our vision with your unique talents and eye for beauty and originality. Thank you for putting into visual art all of what you do.

To Kellie, Curly, Kelly Ann, and Edwina, thank you for always having a heart of gold and for always being in a good mood. You're amazing. You'll always be number one, the OG. To Ed, the bright light who elevated our art of service. The world could use more of your charm, selflessness and kindness. To our core head office team, our pillars that keep the salad train moving right along: Berto for your constant gardening and tending of the Mandy's soil; Lisa for being the sharpest, most brilliant, BTS wizard; Lou for being the inappropriately hilarious one, but also the one who's casually getting her law degree on the side; Andrea for getting our culture so quickly and enmeshing with the extended salad fam from day one. We love you. To Kelsey, the chillest, most culturally-on-point, funniest quasi-daughter, thank you for all that you do, and for feeling like a part of the family right from the start. Tony, Jess, for keeping us all in check—thank you for your loyalty and diligence, and for helping to rein in your crazy boho-boss-sisters' ideas sometimes. To Madda, what would we do without you? Your commitment, loyalty, beauty, and fierce protection of the business and everyone's best interests are one of a kind. We love you, and are grateful for you.

Lachie, you need your own section. I know how much you love the spotlight, so here goes: thank you for sharing the same love of food, for all the texting with recipe ideas, funny toddler story swapping, nerding out on fun facts, your incredible work ethic (so hard to find), and your delicious recipes we have been so proud to feature. Working with you in ANY kitchen is always the bright spot of my day, even when you're grumpy cat, you know I love you . . . almost as much as you love my measuring techniques.

To the incredible location managers who are so committed to delivering excellence, from the back foodies to the front VIP ambassadors, thank you from the bottom of my heart for carrying on the traditions and values that Bec and I put in place so many years ago. You know who you are; I love you and am so grateful for you.

To my Dinner Girlzzz Sianee, Goldie, Moria/Morris, Mamma Myri, Nini, and Nat, thank you for 14 years of being my ride or dies. Your sisterhood, dinners, recipe sharing, 500 group texts a day, tears and laughter mean the world to me.

Belle, thank you for always being one of our biggest fans, forever bonding over our love of *gourmande* everything, giggles, travel, and our biggest shared love: Zaki. To Janis, you are my original rock 'n' roll foodie BFF. Thank you for all things fun, fashion, delicious, and spiritual. I miss you every day. To FACZL, the Mendell-Tremblay posse, thank you for (almost) competing with us for biggest family. Our meals together have always been epic, and our laughter even greater.

To my best friend, rock, and love, my habibi, Mike, and to all our kids—Zak, Jules, Charlie, and Ella— you are my everything. Mike, for your loyalty, support, and love, and accompanying me to Aubut, Costco, and every market back in the early days, slinging trash and recycling out onto the streets at 5 a.m., and for your love to this day of the smell of roasting chicken and sweet sesame syrup reminding us of our early days, too; I love you. You are always home to me, wherever we are. And kids, one day you will love salads, and I will rejoice ;)

To Vince the Prince, the most patient, helpful, supportive, and positive Montreal connector I have ever known. Your heart is limitless. Thank you for believing in us and giving us our start. Teta & Gido, thank you for your warmth from day one, for your strong family values, for your tenderness for the grandkids, and for sharing countless delectable Lebanese meals together.

To Susana, thank you for taking such good care of all of us, our home, and our kids. We would not be able to do it all without you. Thank you for all your loyalty and dedication, we love you.

Joodles, Mommy, our number-one fan and groupie, thank you for all the childhood memories in the kitchen with you, allowing me to taste and play with everything along the way. You're the sweetest, most generous, and classiest woman I know. Your wisdom continues and enriches with every passing year, you've taught me so much, most of all how to be a loving benevolent mom.

Jess, for your heart, endless creativity and wisdom, and for happy memories of crazy partying, eating our way through Europe and Australia in the summers, experiencing so many firsts with you, I love you so much. Josh, you are one fine young man. Thank you for letting me cook for you over the years and licking the cookie dough spoon when you were still my "little" bro. You guys are incredibly lovely people and I am so proud to be your sister.

To Dad, I know you're watching all of this from above, beaming with pride; thank you for our fierce Wolfe Pack family values, for reminding us that "who cares what other people think— be true to you" and instilling the entrepreneurial spirit in us all . . .

Lettuce ladies
supporting charity

Country party
planning

Country
company retreat

Laval opening

OG Office
Xmas party 🩶

The extended Wolfe Pack: Richie, Sonny & Denise, Lynn & Howie, Alyssa, Lolo & Daniel, thank you for some of the happiest childhood memories, be they lakeside up north, on the coast of Maine, or any Jewish High Holiday, our togetherness, riotous laughter, and shared love of food and kids is a part of who I am today. I love you all.

Bex, my other life partner. What a beautiful, mind-blowing trip it's been! Thank God we've got each other. I can't believe I get to "work" with you every day; we are lucky beyond words. You are a creative genius. Thank you for your unique vision that you manifest in our exquisite spaces. The love, respect, and appreciation I have for you knows no bounds. You are one in a million, and I love you more every day.

And finally, to the salad lovers out there, to our die-hard Montreal loyal peeps, the consistent supporters of our journey from way back when: we wouldn't be where we are without all of you—you have changed our lives forever. Thank you for always rooting for us.

REBECCA | Big thanks to Meredith for taking a chance on us with this book. Your experience and finesse in everything food-related has been a true gift throughout this journey. You have a way with words and a keen eye that's been extremely inspiring to work with. Thank you for putting this all together and for making our book dream come true.

Thank you to Alison, Kerrie, and Lachie for all your hard work and diligence in producing some of the most gorgeous food photos out there. Each photo shoot holds memories of laughter and fun creative experiments—the things that make me happiest. Thanks for coming on this journey with us. I hope we can do this over and over again for many books to come. Thank you to Kendra for your impeccable testing, to Lindsay for your editing and belief, and to Sarah as always for your design and just "getting" me.

To my everything partner, thank you for inspiring me to always dream big. You gave me the wings I needed to fly by never doubting me along this journey and always being my number-one fan. I love you, Vince. Thank you to my little munchkins for giving me a reason every day to want to be better, to do better—you are my higher purpose.

Thank you to the entire Mandy's family, without whom none of this would be possible. You make "work" fun every day. Our vision for this journey would be impossible without each and every one of you. We are a people company first and foremost, and working together toward a bigger dream with all of you makes every day extremely fulfilling and motivating.

Mommy, I love you—thanks for teaching me what "trust in the ones you love" means. You've always believed in what I'm doing. I'm forever grateful for your unconditional support in all aspects of my life. Daddy, thank you for instilling an entrepreneurial spirit deep within me. You taught me that no mountain is ever too big, no idea is ever too weird to pursue, and no dream is ever out of reach. And most of all, that perseverance trumps all. I love you.

To my twin, thank you, Josh. Growing up on the family's "young team" with you as my wingman was one of my greatest gifts. You continue to impress me all the time with your expansive quest to better yourself and those around you. I truly believe you can run the world one day. Thank you for your friendship. I love you. Thank you, Jess, for all of your support. You're very much a part of some of my earliest creative projects—be it fashion, music, or art. You always broke creative boundaries, and I'm lucky that when I was growing up, I had you as an example of someone who wasn't ever scared to push the envelope. Love you, xx.

Thank you to the entire Cavallo and Mimi & Coco clan: Tony, Vic, Ani, Chris, Dina, and Nick—thanks for being our biggest supporters, for letting us take flight inside your shops, for never second guessing us, and for always growing together with love. Also for showing me what REAL food culture is (#ItaliansDoItBetter). There's never been a dull moment; love you all. Lucy and Vic, thank you for bringing my favorite human into this world and for being such loving, open-minded parents and grandparents. I've learned so much about the "art of living" through your Italian way of doing things. I love you.

Madda, I've learned so much from you about being a solid rock of a person. Your fierce loyalty and dedication to excellence in everything you do is breathtaking. I love you. We wouldn't be anywhere near where we are today without you running our world (literally) every single day. Thank you for all that you do. Elma, thank you for holding us together, for making this last five years of our lives manageable! You are a secret ninja; a multi-tasker like no other. I have so many things to learn from you. We all adore you—thank you for your huge heart and all that you do.

To my potluck ladies, Dana, Nadia, Lisa, Farnie, Jackie, and Liz, thank you for always being there. Our friendship has witnessed the entire evolution of my salad career. I can't imagine living through this chapter of my life without all of your love, advice, support, and inspiration. May we continue to have life-altering fun and unpredictable adventures all the way into our retirement homes! I love you all.

Buns, thank you for belly-aching laughs, for our travel, and for your appreciation for everything embarrassing and hysterical. Thank you for being a sister, I love you. Michelina, thank you for our sisterhood. For being my vault, my unconditional supporter through everything. Thanks for coming up with our "stress lists" before we knew what meditation was. *Je t'aime.*

Harrison crew, thanks for being my other family. You're one special gang, and I hold each of you so close to my heart. You've all been unbelievably supportive in so many ways along my entire journey. Thanks for being you.

To Jojo, my business confidant and *consigliere*. Thank you for always listening and for opening up my eyes to critical situations with a new, clearer perspective. Your advice is invaluable, and I love being around your big, bright energy. To Sherina, your big beautiful heart is extremely admirable. I cherish all of your love and support, and deeply admire your brain (that operates faster than the speed of light!).

Sonny and Denise, I love you. I feel very grateful you moved back to Montreal and aren't going anywhere! Denise, you are a constant source of food and lifestyle inspiration. Big Sonny, thank you for being such an important father figure, especially after we lost our dad. Our kids are lucky to have you as their "other Grandpa". Lynn, Howie, Lolo, Alyssa,

Daniel, and all your wonderful partners and children—I love you from the bottom of my heart, so grateful we grew up in this big, beautiful extended family.

Mindy, Mind, Mindalina . . . I was avoiding writing this bit because there are no words to describe the amount of love and admiration I have for you. I count my lucky stars all the time that the universe gave me you to pursue this dream with. Your wisdom, REAL kindness, authenticity, and integrity in everything you do is mind blowing. Apart from the quality of person you are, your natural inclinations with food never cease to impress me. I thank you for transforming the definition of what a salad is. You're the most innovative chef I know, one of a kind, Mindle—so proud to call you my other life partner. I love you.

MEREDITH | I would like to thank Mandy and Rebecca for inviting me aboard. After eating some—er, 567,000—Mandy's salads since 2008, I figured I was the right person for the job. You're the easiest people to work with. Thank you for your constant generosity, hard work, and being such agile and fun collaborators. Thank you, Lachlan, for all of your patience and answers. As always, thank you, Kendra McKnight, for your testing work and invaluable opinion. Thank you to Lindsay Paterson for support and editing. Here's to working together more in the future! Thank you to Robert McCullough and Lindsay Vermeulen for believing. Alison Slattery, you are a complete force and the quickest draw in the east. Thank you for your vision. And thank you to Sarah Lazar for your design prowess.

*Us with Meredith (center)*

241

# Index

MANDY'S

Laurier location